D0960290

A Search for God

BOOK I

1942

Compiled by Study Group #1 of the

Association for Research and Enlightenment, Inc.

Virginia Beach, Virginia

Table of Contents

Meditation 5

Cooperation: *Lesson 1* 25

Know Thyself: *Lesson II* 33

What Is My Ideal? *Lesson III* 43

Faith: *Lesson IV* 49

Virtue and Understanding: *Lesson V* 59

Fellowship: *Lesson VI* 69

Patience: *Lesson VII* 81

The Open Door: *Lesson VIII* 91

In His Presence: *Lesson IX* 101

The Cross and the Crown: *Lesson X* 111

The Lord Thy God Is One: *Lesson XI* 125

Love: *Lesson XII* 135

Index and Glossary of Terms 145

This printing of
A Search for God, Book I,
is dedicated to
Elsie Sechrist,
lifelong supporter
of this work.

PREFACE

Try living the precepts of this book.

Here is a unique compilation of information dealing with spiritual laws of daily living. Why is it unique?

The manuscript resulted from the study and work of the original Study Group #1 of the Association for Research and Enlightenment, Incorporated, Virginia Beach, Virginia. It was written not by one person but by many individuals.

The affirmations and basic discourses under each chapter heading came from general readings given by Edgar Cayce. Questions were asked and experiences during meditation explained in subsequent readings for twelve people.

To these individuals it brought hope, peace, a better understanding of their fellow man and an inner joy in a greater awareness of attunement with the Creator.

There is nothing new here. The search for God is as old as man. This book is passed on in the hope that through it, during the trying times ahead, many may glimpse a ray of light; that in other hearts it may awaken a new hope and vision of a better world through application of His laws in daily life.

MEDITATION

"Be still, and know that I am God."

Psalm 46:10

OUTLINE

MEDITATION

I. Introduction

II. Prayer and Meditation

    1. Prayer defined and illustrated

    2. Meditation defined

    3. Will prayer answer for meditation?

III. Preparation for Meditation

    A. *The Physical Body*

        1. A knowledge, cleansing, and consecration of the physical body

        2. A study of the glands

        3. A study of vibrations

    B. *The Mental Body*

        1. The purging of self

        2. The attunement of self to the Whole

    C. *The Spiritual Body*

        1. The soul

        2. The ideal

IV. The Forces

V. Methods of Meditation

VI. Conclusion

Prayer

Our Father which art in HEAVEN,
  Hallowed be thy NAME.
Thy kingdom come. Thy WILL be done in earth,
  as it is in heaven.
Give us this day our daily BREAD.
And forgive us our DEBTS, as we forgive
  our debtors.
And lead us not into TEMPTATION,
  but deliver us from EVIL:
For thine is the KINGDOM, and the POWER,
  and the GLORY, for ever. Amen.

                                    Matthew 6:9-13

MEDITATION

I. Introduction

In this material world we are conscious of the phenomenon of growth. We should be equally aware of spiritual progression that includes both a broadening of understanding of the relation between the Creator and ourselves, and a definite improvement in capacities for more useful lives. Too much stress has been placed upon the desirability of escaping from physical existence. The average individual has come to look upon spiritual things as being intangible and ethereal, unconnected with normal life.

The eternal question that runs through life is this: What is truly valuable in thought, in activity, and in experience? Only from within can come a stable estimate of what is worthwhile. This sense of appreciation or this inner realization is based fundamentally upon an understanding of self—self in relation to others and self in relation to God. Meditation is the means to this end.

II. Prayer and Meditation

1. Prayer defined and illustrated

Some individuals give little thought to either prayer or meditation. They are satisfied to drift with the current, hoping that somehow or somewhere conditions will work out for the best for them. There are others who seek a better way, searching for that light which renews hope, gives a more perfect understanding of their present lot, and justifies the course of life that is being pursued.

Prayer is the concerted effort of our physical consciousnesses to become attuned to the Consciousness of the Creator. It is the attunement of our conscious minds to the spiritual forces that manifest in a material world. It may be a cooperative experience of many individuals, coming together with one accord and with one mind.

Prayer to some is the pouring out of personality for outward show, to be seen by men. To others it means entering into the closet of the inner self and pouring out the ego so that the inner being may be filled with the Spirit of the Father. These divergent attitudes are illustrated in the example drawn by Christ.

> "Two men went up into the temple to pray, the one a Pharisee, and the other a publican. The Pharisee stood and prayed thus with himself, God, I thank thee, that I am not as other men are, extortioners, unjust, adulterers, or even as this publican. I fast twice in the week, I give tithes of all that I possess. And the publican, standing afar off, would not lift up so much as his eyes unto heaven, but smote upon his breast, saying, God be merciful to me a sinner. I tell you, [said Jesus] this man went down to his house justified rather than the other."   *Luke 18:10-14*

2. Meditation defined

Meditation is the emptying of ourselves of all that hinders the Creative Force from rising along the natural channels of our physical bodies to be disseminated through the sensitive spiritual centers in our physical bodies. When meditation is properly entered into, we are made stronger mentally and physically. "He went in the strength of that meat received for many days." (281-13)

Meditation is not musing or daydreaming, but attuning our mental and physical bodies to their spiritual source. It is arousing the mental and spiritual attributes to an expression of their relationship with their Maker. This is true meditation.

Meditation is prayer from within the inner self and partakes not only of the inner physical man but of the soul aroused by the spirit from within. In prayer we speak to God, in meditation God speaks to us.

3. Will prayer answer for meditation?

Will asking a question answer it? No, but it shows that we desire information, and therefore it has its merits. Just so when we pray. We show to our heavenly Father that we are anxious for His guidance and help, for the manifestation of His promises in our lives. It then takes an attitude of waiting, of silence, of listening, to be able to hear the still small voice whisper within, and to know that all is well. Prayer therefore is the basis of meditation.

Only when we are still may we know God, and when we know Him we are willing to say and mean, "Thy will be done." It is then that He sups with us.

In prayer we ask for cleansing; before true meditation we must be clean in body and mind so that we may be fit to meet our Lord. One is a complement of the other.

III. Preparation for Meditation

A. *The Physical Body*

1. A knowledge, cleansing, and consecration of the physical body

We are miniature copies of the universe, possessing physical, mental, and spiritual bodies. These bodies are so closely knit together that the impressions of one have their effects upon the other two. The physical body is a composite unit of creative force manifesting in a material world. So all-inclusive is the physical body that there is nothing in the universe that man can comprehend that does not have its miniature replica within it. It is not only our privilege but our duty to know ourselves, and to be aware of our bodies being temples of the living God.

Individuals have found throughout the ages that preparation is necessary for deep meditation. For some it is necessary that the body be cleansed with pure water, that certain foods or associations (with man or woman) be avoided, and that certain types of breathing be taken so that there may be an even balance in the whole respiratory system. This produces a normal flow of circu-

lation through the body. Others feel that odors, incanta-
tions, sounds, or music are conducive to producing the
best conditions. As the current rises through the centers
in the body, these outer influences may help to cleanse
the thoughts and quiet the mind and body. So-called
savages arouse within themselves the passions or thirst
for destruction through the battle cry or the use of certain
drones or sounds. This is the same force used negatively.
(See 440-12, A-21; 281-13.)

The following is an illustration: An engineer, before
going into an electric power plant for work, must take off
a certain type of wearing apparel and put on another. His
mind must be filled with a thorough knowledge and
understanding of the mechanism to be handled, lest
death and destruction result. How much more is a
cleansing and understanding necessary when we seek to
attune our bodies to the source of all force? He has
promised to meet us within our own sanctuary. He that
goes in unworthily does it to his own destruction.

While the method may not be the same with everyone,
if we would meditate, we must shut ourselves away from
the cares of the world and purify our bodies physically.
"Consecrate yourselves this day," is given in the law,
"that ye may on the morrow present yourselves before
the Lord that He may speak through *you!*" (281-13) as a
father speaketh with his children. Have we wandered so
far away that we dare not await His presence? Do we not
remember He has promised "If ye will be my children I
will be your God" and "Though ye wander far away, if ye
will but call I will hear"? (281-41)

We must find that which to our consciousness is the
best way of purifying body and mind before attempting
to enter into meditation. In raising the image of that
through which we are seeking to know the will of the
Creative Force, actual creation takes place within us.

When we have found a way to cleanse our bodies so
that which is to be raised finds its full measure of
expression within, we can readily understand how
healing of every nature may be disseminated by thought.

When we have cleansed ourselves in the manner that is

to us the best, there will be no fear that our experiences will become so overpowering as to cause any physical or mental disorder. It is when there is no cleansing that entering into such a state brings disaster, or pain, or disease.

2. A study of the glands

When we quiet the physical body through turning the mind toward the highest ideal, there are aroused actual physical vibrations, as a result of spiritual influence becoming active on the sensitive vibratory centers in the body, stimulating the points of contact between the soul and its physical shell. Let us trace this activity.

When we attune ourselves to the Infinite, the glands of reproduction may be compared to a motor which raises the spiritual power in the body. This spiritual power enters through the center of the cells of Leydig glands (located in the genitive system). This center is like a sealed or open door, according to the use to which it has been put through spiritual activities. With the arousing of the image, or ideal, this life force rises along what is known as the Appian Way or the silver cord, to the pineal center in the brain, whence it may be disseminated to those centers that give activity to the whole mental and physical being. It rises then to the hidden eye in the center of the brain system (pituitary body), which is just back of the middle of the forehead. Thus on entering meditation there arises a definite impulse from the glands of reproduction that passes through the pineal to the pituitary gland. Whatever the ideal of an individual is, it is propelled upward and finds expression in the activity of the imaginative forces. If this ideal is material, there is built more and more into the body a love for, and a tendency towards, things of the earth. If this ideal or image is of a spiritual nature there is spiritual development. Psychic forces are only an awakening of soul faculties through activities in these centers. If an anatomical or pathological study should be made for a period of seven years (which is the cycle of change in all body elements), of an individual who is acted upon through the pituitary gland alone, it would be discovered that such a person trained in spiritual laws would become a light to the world. One trained in purely material things would become a Frankenstein [monster], without a concept of any influence other than material or mental. (See 262-20.)

During the rising of the currents along this silver cord and in these centers, a body may become conscious of distinct vibrations. There are three principal motions that correspond to the three-dimensional concept of the conscious mind: namely, the backward and forward, the side to side, and the circular movements. These sensations may be very real. They may cause an apparent vibration or motion in the body itself that is simply a movement within the body, without outward effect. Another very common sensation is that of the current or vibration passing up the spine or through the body from the feet upward, or vice versa. These may also be accompanied or followed by a lightness, or slight dizziness. It may also be pointed out here that the reactions within individuals may differ, for the composite vibrations of a body acted upon by spiritual thought differ in various individuals. The important point is that a definite, physical reaction, in sensitive centers, takes place.

3. A study of vibrations

Before entering further into the discussion of meditation, it would be well to outline a few elementary principles of vibration which will enable us to better understand many of the terms used, and some of the experiences we may have. Science teaches us that all matter is in motion, and that the difference in various forms of matter is due to the difference in the rates of vibration. For example, we know that by increasing the molecular activity of water by heating we can produce another form of matter called steam; that is, the particles of matter in the steam are vibrating (moving) at a faster rate of speed than the particles in water. Now, our bodies are made up of particles of matter which have been taken into them, such as food, air, et cetera. Various parts of our bodies are composed of different types of matter, vibrating at different rates of speed. The nervous system, for example, is highly sensitive. Our bones are of denser structure than our blood, muscular tissue denser than membrane, and so on. The combination of the vibrations of all of these different parts forms a general rate of vibration for the body. This is constantly changing. Illness of any kind causes discordant vibrations. The higher the rate of vibration, the more sensitive the body is to influences of any kind.

As we go deeper in the study of meditation, we become conscious, through application, of these various vibrations in and through the body and mind. As we attempt deep meditation, spiritual forces within and without the body-mind will at first be limited by the five senses of perception, for only through these can we recognize any manifestation in this plane. Even when we have learned to lay the physical aside entirely and explore wider realms, the concepts brought back with us must be clothed in three-dimensional terms to be consciously understood.

Vibrations which are emanations of life from within are material expressions of a spiritual influence, a force that emanates from life itself. When a vibration arises, it may act only upon centers within the human body that are sensitive to vibrations, else they may not become apparent. These, spiritualized, are emanations which may be sent out as thought waves, as a force in the activity of universal or cosmic influence, and thus have their effect upon those toward whom, by suggestion, they are directed. (See 281-7, A-14; 281-12, A-12.)

Let us consider the effect of thought upon the body in relation to vibration. All thoughts are constructed at different vibratory rates. As the food we take into the body is important from the standpoint of structure, so thoughts are important as factors that build up the mental pattern. Mind is the builder. It is the construction engineer that molds even the actual physical matter in its higher vibratory forms. We should therefore never use

thought vibrations by attempting to make ourselves
other than a channel to help others.

B. *The Mental Body*

1. The purging of self

Let us consider what takes place in the mental body
during meditation. The mind is the builder, the physical
the result. The mind partakes of both the physical and
the spiritual. Most of us are aware of only a part of the
mind; this we call the conscious mind. Even in the field of
psychology, recent investigations have revealed little
beyond a bare glance at what is called the subconscious,
the storehouse of memory and the ever-watchful super-
visor of the regular functions of the body. There is still
another division of the mind. This may be called the activity of the superconscious, or soul-mind. (These are
only names that we use in trying to clarify for our imperfect understanding the meanings of different functions of one force.)

Through meditation we seek to allow our mind to function normally. Through the will we ask the mind of our
physical bodies to cease its wanderings and center itself
upon the ideal, which will be presented to the higher
mind. This ideal becomes the basis for the activity which
results.

If the ideal and purpose we hold are in accord with the
superconscious mind, that which will be of help and
value to the physical mind and body will be transmitted
into consciousness through some channel of the five
senses. Proof of this higher mental activity will come to
each of us as he seeks to understand. If, however, the
ideal and purpose are out of harmony with the soul-mind,
the opening of the door between the physical and
spiritual will result in turmoil within, striking at the
weakest point.

So it is necessary to purify our minds if we would meditate. Think of what we should do to have our God meet us
face to face. Would we say, "Many are not able to speak to

God, many are fearful"? (281-41) Have we gone so far astray that we cannot approach Him who is all merciful? He knows our desires and needs, yet He can supply us only according to the purposes within ourselves.

Then let us purify our bodies, our minds, and consecrate ourselves in prayer. Let us put away from us hate, greed, and malice, and replace them with love and mercy. Let there be in our hearts humbleness, for we must humble ourselves if we would know Him. Let us come with an open, seeking, contrite heart desiring to have the way shown us. Then let us seek to enter.

2. The attunement of self to the Whole

Attunement depends upon soul development. Physically, the radio may be an illustration. The attunement on any radio may be somewhere near the same point of another, but on no two, even when sitting side by side, will it be the same, for the position of the sets alters that. So in attuning our consciousness to the Divine, each of us must make the attunement according to his own development. Attunement, like all attainments in creation, is a growth. "In my Father's house are many mansions [states of consciousness]...I go and prepare a place for you...that where I am [in consciousness], there ye may be also [in consciousness]."[1]

Proper attunement is necessary for true meditation. A perfect attunement may be made with the Ideal, the Infinite, when we make our minds and our wills one with His in word, action, intent, and purpose. Let us pray, "Father, not my will but Thine be done in and through me," (262-3) and mean it.

How may we know we are not in attunement? It is when we have lost interest in our fellow man. To be out of harmony with our brother is to be out of harmony with our Maker. Does not the Bible say, "If thou bring thy gift to the altar, and there remembereth that thy brother hath ought against thee; Leave there thy gift before the altar, and go thy way; first be reconciled to thy brother, and then come and offer thy gift."[2] "Thou shalt love the Lord

[1] John 14:2, 3   [2] Matt. 5:23, 24

thy God with all thy heart . . . and thy neighbour as thyself."[3]

C. *The Spiritual Body*

1. The soul

It is through meditation that we may become aware of the existence of the spiritual forces within, that we unlock the door between our physical and spiritual bodies. Through this door come impulses from the soul, seeking expression in the physical.

Our souls are endowed with many faculties that are limited and bound by our impressions in the physical. The soul is always present, always willing to express its true purpose, its true relationship with the Creator. Through meditation we make this possible; we open the way.

Some say that we are not conscious of possessing a soul. We should know that each of us is a soul. This body in which we live is only our house for the moment, and then out of it we go on to other states of consciousness and other experiences.

The fact that we hope, that we have desires for better things, that we are able to be sorry or glad, indicates activities of the mind that take hold upon something that is not temporal in nature, something that does not pass away at the death of the body. Such mental activities come from the spiritual center of our being, the soul. God breathed the breath of life into man and he became a living soul.[4]

Then, each is a soul endowed with the attributes of God, possessing the power of creation, of being one with the Father, a joint heir with the Son.

2. The ideal

There are as many types of meditation as there are individuals who meditate. For some it is an escape from the trials of the world; for others it is an access to knowledge; for still others it is an approach to God. Various forms of meditation exist, each with its adherents. But

[3]Luke 10:27   [4]See Genesis 2:7

the real significance is in the ideal and purpose. The sweetest incense or the most beautiful music will not lift a selfish heart into the presence of the Creator. It is much more important that our minds be free of malice, hate, greed, and selfishness, than that some complex form for meditation be observed. Let us not become involved and confused by material means to meditation, but rather consider first the fundamental reason for it and make that reason in harmony with the highest desire we can conceive.

There are definite changes that take place within us when we enter into true or deep meditation. There is physical activity, through the imaginative or impulsive powers. The sources of impulse are aroused by shutting out thoughts pertaining to activities or attributes of carnal forces. Changes naturally take place when there is an arousing of those stimuli within us which have the seat of the soul as a home. If the ideal, the image, the mark of a high calling, is a standard which is in accord with the highest aspiration of service which we can recognize, then we bear the mark of the Lamb, the Christ. As we raise this, we are able to enter into the very presence of the Creative Force. (See 281-13.)

Some of us have so overshadowed ourselves by abuses of the mental attributes of the body that only an imperfect image may be raised within.

If our aims of meditation are only to still the physical, the direct method should be used. But this is not usually the case. A higher state of spiritual consciousness is the aim and purpose of deep meditation. It is important, therefore, that attention be fixed upon the ideal which is to be raised. The physical quiet of the human organism will follow as a natural result, and there will be a growth of unity, of inner feeling, rather than separate, broken points of consciousness. Now, in fixing attention upon the ideal there should be created a desire to reach the highest possible state of awareness of which the whole being is capable. This does not mean fixation upon the words of an affirmation, but a strong desire that the meeting with the inner self and God be unobstructed and unmarred by other distractions. The quieting of the body should result from an inner spiritual effort rather than from a fixation of consciousness on outer stimuli.

IV. The Forces

In meditation, more than at any other time, we become conscious of the forces. We refer to them as psychic, occult, intuitive, universal, and so on. These are only names designating the various functions of God. "Hear, O Israel: the Lord our God is one Lord."[5]

Let us consider, for an example, intuitive force that arises from experiences of our whole being. It can be developed by introspective activities of our conscious mind, until it is able to bring to bear such experiences upon our daily lives. We call this "entering into the silence."[6]

Those who by constant introspection are able to bring to the surface their experiences as a whole are called "sages" or "lamas." When this ability is made practical by an individual and yet remains spiritual in aspect, such an individual becomes a master.

There is much to be gained in the study of the forces through meditation, introspection, or entering into the silence. It is well to have a thorough knowledge of the subject, but never pretend to be mysterious about it. Jesus lived simply, doing good among His fellow men.

As we, in meditation, open ourselves to the unseen forces that surround the throne of grace, beauty, and might within ourselves, let us throw around us the protection found in the thought of the Christ. When our minds are on God, the Christ, who is our Ideal, we need not worry about destructive results. Remember the promise, "Behold, I stand at the door, and knock: if any man hear my voice, and open the door, I will come in to him, and will sup with him, and he with me."[7] "It is I; be not afraid."[8]

It is when we hold the right ideal that our problems are solved and stumbling blocks become stepping-stones.

[5]Deut. 6:4   [6]P.R.   [7]Rev. 3:20   [8]Matt. 14:27

V. Methods of Meditation

We must learn to meditate just as we learn to walk or talk or to develop any physical attribute.

We must direct our consciousness through desire, controlled by will.

The following suggestions are offered as an outline that may be used by each individual. We are all capable of choosing the form that is most pleasing, most suitable, and most fitting for us as individuals. Our various developments fit us to accept and understand different forms. For some, the simplest approach is the best; for others, a complicated procedure is necessary. There must be a spiritual intent and purpose, a true desire to seek His will, not ours, as we enter in. God is spiritual force and must be sought through a spiritual ideal, set by Him who perfected the way, and who thus became the Way. Let His principles be the guide in the formation of the ideal, the image, that is raised within.

Cleanse the body with pure water. Sit or lie in an easy position, without binding garments about the body. Three times breathe in through the right nostril and exhale through the mouth; three times breathe in through the left nostril and exhale through the right nostril. Then, either with the aid of low music or an incantation which carries the self deeper into a sense of oneness with the creative forces of love, enter into the Holy of Holies. As self feels or experiences the raising of this, see it disseminated through the inner eye (not carnal eye) to that which will bring the greater understanding in meeting every condition in the experience of the body. Then, we may listen to the music that is made as each center of the body responds to the new Creative Force that is being disseminated, each through its own channel. We will find that, little by little, meditation will enable us to renew ourselves physically, mentally, and spiritually. (See 281-28, A-1.)

Experiences

1. In meditation some individuals experience a vibra-

tory sensation which seems to move the body from side to side, or backward and forward. This may become a circular motion within the body, bringing a fullness and whirling sensation in the head.

2. Other individuals feel a coolness upon the head and forehead.

3. Some sense a pulsation in the lower part of the spine. This may come from nerve impulses flowing through the body from the lower genitive centers to other gland centers which control various activities of the physical body. Let us not force these, but so conduct our minds and the activities of our bodies as to leave ourselves channels for such expressions.

4. Others experience a vibration running up through the body and ending in a sensation of fullness in the head. When we are able to raise within ourselves vibrations that pass through the whole course of the attributes of physical attunements to the disseminating center, or spiritual eye, then our bodies become magnets that may, if properly used, bring healing to others, with a laying on of hands.

5. A sensation to the eyes is indicative of a healing vibration. Healing of every sort must come first in self before it can be raised in another.

6. A voice speaking to an individual is a manifestation of an awakening within self of the abilities to associate, connect, and communicate with those influences from without self. Then, as given of old, if there will be held and magnified within the consciousness of self the desire for that Voice, that Presence, which would aid in bringing the various consciousnesses to self, the experiences will be from the universal influences or from His messenger. Magnify this in self and for self. Be mindful that it is not clothed in some other power.

7. Then, finally, there is the passing into the presence of that which may materialize in voice, feeling, sight, and a consciousness of oneness with the Whole.

VI. Conclusion

If self-development is our aim, then we must begin just

where we are. It will do no good idly to wish to be in some other condition or surrounding; for, unless we have mastered our present state, the second will be worse than the first. The first and last obstacle to overcome is understanding ourselves. Until we are fully aware of all that constitutes our existence we have no right to say that this or that is the aim and goal of life. Our capacities and abilities are of the highest creation. Let us not fool ourselves by accepting anything but the fullest expression of consciousness.

Meditation is the safest and surest way to understand ourselves. It is the key to the door which is closed on the real world for most of us. Let us study and know ourselves. It is a command, an entreaty. Let us dare to seek, not blindly, but with faith, that we may find "the noble self." (See 281-7, A-11-14.) Our approaches and results may differ, but the same understanding, the same point of consciousness, and the same state of awareness are the ultimate goals. Two attitudes are essential:

1. A strong desire to seek truth.

2. A constant, consistent effort to move forward.

Let us be continuous and regular in meditation. Broken periods of meditation will accomplish little. Be active in holding the ideal, and be regular in awakening the inner self.

In the end, the reward is well worth the effort expended. Most of us waste hours each day when just a few moments spent in daily search within would bring more peace and joy, and more true happiness, than any physical activity. Then let us first seek the kingdom of heaven. Where is the kingdom of heaven? It is within. What He gave of old is as true today as it was in the beginning. Let us call on Him and know that our bodies are temples of the living God. There He has promised to meet us.

Are we afraid? Are we ashamed? Have we so belittled our opportunities, have we so defamed our own bodies and our own minds that we are ashamed to have our God meet us within our tabernacles? If such is the case, let us set our houses in order.

There are spiritual centers in our bodies which are points of physical contact between the physical organism and the soul. These connections are just as real as the nerve centers and fibers which carry impulses from one of the sense organs to the brain. There is a bowl that must one day be broken, and a cord that must one day be severed from the physical body of each individual.[9] The ultimate goal of each soul's searching is a greater awareness of God. Through meditation we may increase this awareness in daily life and prepare the way for the change called death to bring us another step forward toward the goal.

What is our God? Are we ambitious only as to whether we shall eat tomorrow or as to wherewithal we shall be clothed? We are of little faith and of little hope who allow such to become the paramount issues in our consciousness. Know we not that we are His? We are of His making. He has willed that we shall not perish, but has left it with us as to whether we become even aware of our relationships with Him. In our houses, our bodies, there are ways for the approach—through the desire to know Him. We put that desire into activity by purging our bodies and our minds of those things that we know, or even conceive of, as being hindrances. It has been given of old that it was not for those who would descend from heaven to bring us a message, or those who would come from over the seas, but that we would find Him within our own hearts and consciousnesses.

Would we ask God to do for us what we would not do for our brother? If we would, we are selfish and cannot know God, for as we do it unto the least of our brethren, we do it unto our Maker. These are not mere words—they can be experiences, if we seek to know Him. He is not past finding out. If we would know Him, we must turn to Him; look, hope, and act in such a way that we expect Him, our God, to meet us face to face. "It is I; be not afraid,"[10] said He who came to those seeking to know their relationship with their Maker.

9See Eccles. 12:6   10Matt. 14:27

Many of us become afraid because of the things that we hear, and we say, "I do not understand, I do not comprehend." Why? Have we so belittled ourselves, our bodies, our minds, and our consciousnesses that we have seared and made of no effect those opportunities within us to know our Maker?

Let us purify our bodies and our minds. Let us consecrate ourselves in prayer. Let there be humbleness in our hearts, for we must humble ourselves if we would know Him, and come with an open, seeking, contrite spirit, desirous of having the way shown to us.

When we are shown the way, let us not turn away, but be true to the vision that is given us. He will speak, for His promise has been "When ye call I will hear and will answer speedily."[11] Then when He speaks, let us open our hearts and our minds to the opportunities and glories that are ours. We can accept them through attuning our consciousnesses to the Christ Consciousness in meditation. Then we can say and mean it, "Let others do as they may, but as for us, we will worship—yea, we will serve—the living God."[12]

Even in those times of greatest trial He is not far from us. He is closer than our right hand. He stands at the door of our hearts. Will we bid Him enter, or will we turn Him away? (See 281-41.)

[11]P.R. See Psalm 102:2   [12]P.R. See Joshua 24:15

Lesson I

COOPERATION

"Finally, be ye all of one mind, having compassion one of another; love as brethren." I Peter 3:8

Affirmation

Not my will but Thine, O Lord, be done in me and through me. Let me ever be a channel of blessings, today, now, to those that I contact in every way. Let my going in, my coming out be in accord with that Thou would have me do, and as the call comes, "Here am I, send me, use me."   *262-3*

I

COOPERATION

[Based on Edgar Cayce readings 262-1 through 262-5]

Introduction

Cooperation in the physical is defined as acting or operating jointly with others, concurring with others in action or effort. In the spiritual it is more. It is losing sight of self and becoming a channel through which blessings may flow to others. The blessing is cooperation in action. Whether in the spiritual or physical, action is necessary to put cooperation into operation—thus those who would come together for a common cause must have united action in the pursuit and realization of a common end.

The best in life is ours, not at the expense of others, but in harmonious cooperation. In every successful organization the law is in effect. The heavens declare the Hand which formed them was the Hand of unity, order, and harmony. All nature follows the same law. Each part of the human body performs its duty without a thought of the other, yet fully depending each upon the other.

When self is lost in the Ideal, cooperation is the natural result. It is the natural consequence of self-service, self-sacrifice, self-bewilderment in Him.

In whatever state we find society, let us meet it upon its own level; as we look up, we lift it. That is cooperation.

Need for Cooperation

We must put cooperation into action in our thinking.

Our adverse thoughts have such a paralyzing effect that they will not only retard our own development, but also will build barriers for those who might seek to aid us. The Master could do no mighty works in His own village because of the people's unbelief in Him. Thoughts are deeds and may become crimes or miracles in their application. It is necessary for the accomplishment of any aim, for the reaching of any goal, and for the attainment of any blessing for self or mankind that we have one mind, one aim, and one purpose.

As we seek, in our way, to cooperate in being of service to others, we are lifted up. Let us, then, express the Creative Force within us in such a way that it may bring hope, peace, and understanding into the lives of others, that they too, in their way, may seek to be channels of blessings.

Then, let us attune ourselves to the highest spiritual Force. This will come when we are in accord with His will.

Let us exercise our conscious mind by holding these two thoughts before us:

1. We must lose ourselves in Him.

2. Our every thought and our every deed must be in harmony with the intent and purposes of the best that is within us.

What is the mind of the Christ that we should seek?

As we open our minds, our hearts, and our souls, that we may be channels of blessings, we then have the mind of the Christ, who took upon Himself the burden of the world. So may we, in our little spheres, take upon ourselves the burdens of our world. The joy, peace, and happiness that may be ours are found in doing for the other fellow. Gaining an understanding of the laws that pertain to right living in all its phases makes our minds in attune with Creative Forces. (See *A Search for God*, Book II, p. 82.) We have the mind of Christ of putting into action that which we know.

Method of Obtaining Cooperation

Now, the questions arise: How may we accomplish this? How may we work as individuals whose purposes will be in accord with His will? To answer these we must look within to the little things that go to make up our very nature. We must guard our daily thoughts and acts, and must, through meditation, awaken our inner selves.

In the daily walk of life let us take stock of our thoughts and acts, for cooperation is the offering of self to be a channel of activity, of thought. It is not attained at once, but comes line upon line, precept upon precept, through the giving of self. We must realize that they who would have life must give life; they who would have love must show themselves lovable; they who would have friends must be friendly; they who would have cooperation must cooperate by giving self to that which is to be accomplished, whether in bringing light, strength, health, or understanding to others. These are one in Him.

Let us replace our negative thoughts with positive ones, thinking not unkindly of anyone but speaking and thinking kindly of all. Let us practice thinking kind thoughts of those who have hurt us, letting no opportunity pass to do a little act of kindness that will lighten the burden of another. We should live as we know He would have us live. Begin now. Work! Work diligently and consistently. Let us take thought continually of the attitude of mind we hold; for it makes for that which gives birth to peace, harmony, and understanding; or it brings forth the contending forces that make for unrest and trouble. We will find, when we would do right, that the spirit of unrest is ever present; but day by day this should be put out of our minds and more and more replaced by thoughts of peace, harmony, and understanding—not a latent kind, but an active force. This is the manner in which we give expression to that being sought.

It is a oneness of mind, a oneness of purpose, which we must all seek; the virtue in the knowledge of God—His laws, His precepts—not to the advantage of self, but for others; not for self-edification, but that power and strength may emanate from us to others less strong. Let us seek harmony, for harmony makes for peace, and peace makes for understanding, and understanding for enlightenment.

We of ourselves can do nothing; so let us, in meditation, seek the knowledge of the inner Light. Set aside a time each day for prayer and meditation, preferably at sunrise; quiet the physical body, purify the emotions, and wait on the Lord. Let us draw nigh unto God and He will draw nigh unto us.

As we enter into meditation, let us visualize the force of harmony and love in action. As we put into practice that which we know of cooperation in deed and in thought, there will come to us His peace which passes understanding, and the realization of being His channel. He has promised that power, strength, joy, life, and light will not be withheld from those who seek this oneness in His name.

Realization of Cooperation

As the realization of a perfect cooperation in Him comes to us, there will come also the knowledge of our oneness with the Creative Force of the universe. Self-interest will be eliminated. Joy and happiness, found in service, will reign in our hearts. Our bodies and our minds will function more perfectly, because the Creative Force, which ever seeks expression in all, has been aroused in us. Understanding will come as quietly as the silent shadows of night, and His everlasting peace will live in our hearts.

There is perhaps no better way to illustrate this realization than to quote a few of the experiences of those who have sought light and understanding through cooperation.

"In experiencing cooperation I have been led into a greater field of spiritual understanding and realize that I am a channel through which His will may be done."

"I experienced in my trials a feeling of cooperation from our study group, in that through their prayers and meditations I realized that nothing but good could come to me. All fear was allayed. I knew that justice and mercy would prevail. There came to me a feeling of contentment, a willingness to leave all in His hands, and a realization that all was well."

"With the cooperation of our study group, I have been better able to understand my own individual purpose in relation to the whole purpose of life. At times, when our cooperation was greatest, I have been able to feel myself being a perfect channel through which God manifested. During the nights following such attunements, I have had visions and dreams that were testimonies to me of growth and development."

"I have realized that faithful repetition of efforts which make for cooperation brings at times a feeling of unity with all with whom I work, and a nearness of His presence, which shows that His promise, 'Where two or three are gathered together in My name, there am I in the midst of them,'[1] is sure."

"In my meditation I have seen our study group come together and form a complete circle, each member of the group being represented by a dot. Each one in the circle seemed to call the others by name and bless them. The circle now turned to a wheel, the dots becoming spokes. Each spoke represented a member of the group. Each spoke became a channel, leading outward from the hub, where was seen the Christ Light. As the blessings of love, harmony, peace, and understanding flowed from the Christ through the channels, the wheel was able to turn. This was cooperation in action. As the wheel revolved, members of the group or channels were able to turn other wheels, which were helping to bring the world to light, love, harmony, and true understanding."

These are the goals for each of us to reach in our varied experiences: unity of purpose, oneness of mind—in that His will, not ours, nor our personalities, may be manifested in all that we do and teach.

Let us be patient and untiring in seeking this cooperation, for we will be preparing ourselves to go on in the study and understanding of spiritual forces, and will

[1] Matt. 18:20

become active channels for these higher forces. We will be better husbands, better wives, better neighbors, and better friends. The little world in which we live will be happier for our being a part of it. We will bring more joy and happiness to those about us and will be manifesting God's love for man.

The way is being opened for all who will to have a part in the redemption of mankind. We must keep our hearts singing, not in sorrow but in gladness of purpose, for of all those chosen of Him we should be the happiest. May our united efforts go through the ages to those yet unborn, regenerating them to that awakening which makes the souls of men safe in the knowledge of Him who made all things, for "without him was not any thing made that was made."[2]

> Not my will but Thine, O Lord, be done in me and through me. Let me ever be a channel of blessings, today, now, to those that I contact in every way. Let my going in, my coming out be in accord with that Thou would have me do, and as the call comes, "Here am I, send me, use me."   *262-3*

[2]John 1:3

Lesson II

KNOW THYSELF

"Now ye are the body of Christ, and members in particular." 1 Corinthians 12:27

Affirmation

Father, as we seek to see and know Thy face, may we each, as individuals and as a group, come to know ourselves, even as we are known, that we—as lights in Thee—may give the better concept of Thy Spirit in this world.   *262-5*

II

KNOW THYSELF

[Based on Edgar Cayce readings 262-5 through 262-11]

Introduction

When we are asked the question "Do you know yourself?" why is it that we cannot answer "Yes"? Within each of us there are certainly great storehouses of abilities and capacities which we have never used. If they were manifested, we would see ourselves in a different light. We would understand the real functions of our physical bodies in relation to our mental and spiritual bodies. Until we are better acquainted with ourselves, we are barriers in the way of our own development.

Each of us must first know that we must set a standard of measurement, of valuation, of precept, and of concept. Let us not measure by earthly standards, if we would know ourselves. Rather, let us measure by that which we have found within ourselves to be our ideal, knowing what we believe in, and acting that way. Let us, therefore, be willing to be measured; not by what we have, but by what we give.

The Physical Body

To know ourselves is not only to be cognizant of the acts of our physical bodies, but to know ourselves as entities, complete factors, capable of knowing all that goes on within and without. This spring of knowledge is tapped only by those who are willing to pay the price. The price is a complete surrender of ourselves, with a purification and a dedication that come only through prayer, meditation, and service. It is along the straight and narrow way, but it is open to all. The water of life is offered freely.

As entities, we are miniature copies of the universe, possessing physical, mental, and spiritual bodies. These bodies are so closely associated and related that the vibrations of one affect the other two. Our mental, especially, partakes of the other two: in the physical, as the conscious mind, and in the spiritual, as the super-conscious mind.

Our bodies are temples of the living God. It has pleased God to so manifest Himself in the world. Our physical bodies are composite units of Creative Force manifesting in the material world. All parts of our bodies must work in unison, for should one war against another, discord would naturally follow. Each part has its functions, and it is so important that no other part can take its place; neither can any part be counted insignificant and useless.

Each organ has its individual functions and desires, which are in themselves holy. The senses make us conscious of the magnified desires or natures of our physical bodies. These are registered in the activities of our physical bodies in such a way that they are stamped upon our very faces. These senses are attuned to the physical, each vibrating according to the training and concentration of the physical forces, seeking expression of the inner self—of which our physical bodies are material representations. For not only do the impressions received through the senses show forth that which is magnified in a single appearance or experience, but also all impressions that have been received through all of our experiences, the registering being in our souls. These are registered in a material way in our physiognomy.

The Mental and Spiritual Bodies

In the same manner the desires of our mental and spiritual bodies build our individualities. This process of building has been going on for ages. The great factors of heredity, environment, karma, thought vibration, and the action of universal laws in the planes beyond the physical all have their influences, just as the desires and vibrations of the physical organs attract and build the composition of the physical body. We are the results not only of the development of the race before us but also of our individual development that has been going on since our creation as individual souls.

We are the sum total of all our experiences in every state of consciousness. "In my Father's house are many mansions"[1] (states of consciousness). In our body temples we are building, by thoughts and acts, not only our physical bodies, but the mental and spiritual bodies as well. Christ, the Master, said: "Not that which goeth into the mouth defileth a man; but that which cometh out of the mouth, this defileth a man."[2] Those of us who live to gratify only our fleshly bodies may be beautiful without, but we have so starved our souls that we are able to give out only that which makes for discord and corruption. In speaking of the scribes and Pharisees, Jesus said: "For ye are like unto whited sepulchres, which indeed appear beautiful outward, but are within full of dead men's bones, and of all uncleanness. Even so ye also outwardly appear righteous unto men, but within ye are full of hypocrisy and iniquity."[3] The same principle may be applied to right thinking, for we become what we think.

The soul will seek that which it has builded, not only in the material plane but in the universal, for "as a tree falls, so will it lie."[4] This is well understood if we know and study ourselves, for we will realize that each experience is a lesson to help bring the knowledge of the Whole, that "I and my Father are one."[5]

When we are seeking to lose ourselves in the Whole, it is possible to see ourselves as did the individual who had the following dream:

"I saw myself pass out of my body and become three bodies, physical, mental, and spiritual. At first the physical was the largest, but as the other two grew it gradually became smaller, until it finally faded into dust.

[1]John 14:2   [2]Matt. 15:11   [3]Matt. 23:27, 28   [4]Eccles. 11:3
[5]John 10:30

The others then grew larger and moved around fourth-dimensionally."

When our acts and thoughts are measured by the standard of Christ, and when we reach the place where we desire only to be channels of blessings to others, we have lost sight of ourselves. Then we have the mind of Christ, for He came not to be ministered to, but to minister, and gave His life as a ransom for many.

Self in Relation to Others

We should let neither flattery, criticism, nor opinions of others turn us aside from those vital things for which we stand—those things that are lifting us upward and building within us that which will endure until the end. Let us turn within to see if we are being true to ourselves when temptations arise. We know that we cannot be true to others unless we are first true to ourselves.

As we cultivate the ability to discriminate between right and wrong, good and evil, we are reaching the plane where we may be masters of our destiny. It is found in keeping the whole law: "Thou shalt love the Lord thy God with all thy heart . . . and thy neighbour as thyself."[6] This is a spiritual desire, for the carnal mind is envious. There is in all of us that still Voice that teaches sacrifice, love, and service, that warns of every catastrophe and protects from all danger. When it is listened to and followed, no mistakes are made, no wars are fought, no homes are broken up; for then we seek the good of our neighbors and the will of the Creator.

Let us dare to see ourselves as others see us. It is well to stand aside and see ourselves go by. Let us think back over the words and acts of the day, asking ourselves these questions: Why did we do this or that? Would we have acted before our God in the manner we acted before our brother? Are we expressing our concepts of God in our lives to those we contact? It is indeed true that "No man liveth to himself and no man dieth to himself."[7]

It is well to know what the other fellow thinks of us. We must, without any feeling of shame or humiliation, be willing to be measured by the standard that we have

[6]Luke 10:27   [7]P.R. See Romans 14:7

given him the impression we hold. It is our duty to study and discipline ourselves so that each word and each action may reflect just what we would be, and not let them be so different that they are not recognized as children of the same family.

While we are seeking to know ourselves through meditation or by taking an inventory, we are passing, as it were, signposts. We see a little light day by day, or catch a word here, an idea there, from those we contact, who help us to realize that all are traveling along the same road. Truly, the better we know ourselves, the better we understand others. Does it not make us more tolerant of our brother if we see him as we are, or as we have been?

Since service is the means of fulfilling our mission here, the question will naturally arise, "Who is this brother that we should serve?" It is he who is in need of help, whether he be friend or foe, regardless of his race or creed. When Jesus defined this question, He said: "Behold my mother and my brethren! For whosoever shall do the will of my Father which is in heaven, the same is my brother, and sister, and mother."[8] If we measure our activities in the daily walks of life by the standard of the Christ, there will never be a regret. It is following the teachings of the Master that will lead more and more in the way toward a perfect understanding.

"Be what you seem. Live your creed. Hold up to earth the torch divine. Be what you pray to be made. Let the Master Jesus' steps be thine."[9]

Self in Relation to Creative Force

By keeping in touch with the Creative Force, we rise above the conditions where the blind lead the blind, and we know that we are guided by the All-Seeing Eye in all we are called to do.

"If I ascend up into heaven, thou art there; if I make my bed in hell, behold, thou art there. If I take the wings of the morning, and dwell in the uttermost parts of the sea; even there shall thy hand lead me."
Psalm 139:8-10

[8]Matt. 12:49-50   [9]P.E.

Let us awake and know that God is speaking to us,
leading us, and protecting us—that His Spirit is even
now bearing witness with our spirit that we are sons of
God.

As the voices of our souls cry out to their Creator, let us
not doubt the promise: "He that hungers and thirsts after
righteousness shall be filled."[10] It may come as the wind,
we may not know from whence, but all who seek will
know that His name is "I am that I am"[11] who is speaking in His holy temple, the body. That is the true awakening. There is, indeed, a physical body, a mental body,
and a spiritual body, and they are one—one in love, one
in truth, one in service, and one in Him.

The Awakening of Self

Our physical bodies, our mental bodies, and our soul
bodies are but shadows of the Triune. The body-physical
is as man. The body-mental is as the savior of man, for it
is through the application of the mental influences that
we would control and build that which finds expression
in the physical and in the soul. The body-soul is made in
the image of the Creator, and made to be a companion in
spirit. The physical body is the house, the home of the
soul, during a sojourn in the material world. What we do
with the opportunities that are presented in our various
experiences gives expression to those powers that are
lent to our souls and our bodies in their passage through
the earth.

As the knowledge of the awakening of our soul forces is
applied in our relationship to our fellow man, we come to
realize our relationship to our Maker, for "As ye do it unto
one of the least of these, ye do it unto Me."[12]

For us to be aware of our physical desires and appetites
is physical awakening. To satisfy them selfishly is sin.
This is illustrated in the experience of our first parents.
"And when the woman saw that the tree was good for
food, and that it was pleasant to the eyes, and a tree to be
desired to make one wise, she took of the fruit thereof, and
did eat, and gave also unto her husband with her; and he
did eat."[13]

[10]P.R. See Matt. 5:6   [11]Exodus 3:14   [12]P.R. See Matt. 25:40
[13]Genesis 3:6

When we become aware that the mind can control the physical desires, then we have a mental awakening. "But Daniel purposed in his heart that he would not defile himself with ... the king's meat, nor with the wine which he drank."[14] This is an illustration of one who stood firm in the light of a mental awakening, even though it was seemingly a sacrifice of life itself.

When we are conscious that we can reconcile the spirit within with the spirit without and know that they are one and are from the same source, God, then we have a spiritual awakening. This was manifested perfectly in Jesus, the Master, in His daily life among men.

An awakening is the natural thing, when we attune ourselves to the Source of all good, allowing His Spirit to bear witness with our spirit. We are awakened then to the knowledge that we are, indeed, sons of God. We show forth our spiritual awakening by our patience, tolerance, long-suffering, and forbearance, not being willing that any should suffer, but that all should come to the knowledge of the Truth. When we practice these virtues in our daily lives we become masters among men.

Conclusion

Let us realize that we should so live in body and in mind that we may be channels through which the Creative Forces may flow. Let us give more attention to our thoughts, for thoughts are deeds and are children of the union of the mind and the soul. What we think continually we become. What we cherish in our minds is built into our own physical bodies, becoming not only food for our souls, but also the soul's heritage in realms of other experiences.

Will is an attribute of the soul. We must recognize by exercising it that we either make ourselves one with our Maker, or separate ourselves from Him. With the will we can either adhere to or contradict those immutable laws set between the Creator and the created.

Let us determine within ourselves that a constructive program will be followed. The conditions of this program, then, require that a definite stand be taken by

[14]Daniel 1:8

each of us. We are determined that we will adhere to it, no matter what we may suffer mentally or physically. We will trust in the divine Force within for the strength to endure and for the ability to say no when we should. We will consider the needs of others before our own.

May we study to show ourselves approved unto God in body, mind, and soul. May we become less and less aware of the desires to gratify the carnal forces of the body. Is our purpose in life to gain power, position, wealth, and to satisfy the longings of the flesh? Are we to lose our own souls by so doing? It is for us to choose. The Christ stands ready to help. Shall we bar the door of our own consciousness?

> Father, as we seek to see and know Thy face, may we each, as individuals and as a group, come to know ourselves, even as we are known, that we—as lights in Thee—may give the better concept of Thy Spirit in this world.   *262-5*

Lesson III

WHAT IS MY IDEAL?

"Let this mind be in you, which was also in Christ Jesus."   Philippians 2:5

Affirmation

God, be merciful to me! Help Thou my unbelief! Let me
see in Him that Thou would have me see in my fellow
man. Let me see in my brother that I see in Him whom I
worship.   *262-11*

III

WHAT IS MY IDEAL?

[Based on Edgar Cayce readings 262-11 through 262-14]

Introduction

What is an ideal? We are told that a mental concept or that conceived as a standard of perfection is an ideal. Mind is the builder. We are ever striving toward something to worship or something to love, be it physical, mental, or spiritual. From our experiences we form ideas; then through the action of imagination we sometimes confuse these ideas with ideals. An ideal is something beyond and above us toward which we build. To bind ourselves by calling our ideas ideals means the beginning of decay in the soul structure which we have builded. Our ideals are ever present; they are either consciously or unconsciously the bases for the motivating forces in our lives.

Ideals Grow with Development

In childhood the height which we hoped to reach was lower, by far, than the one that we placed as a goal in youth. We recall that the God we worshiped in our childhood has grown to the Spirit we now call "Abba, Father."[1] So, as we build onward and upward, our ideals enlarge until they reach the height of perfection, the Source of all Good, the Creative Energy of which we are manifestations.

From the physical, mental, and spiritual viewpoints our ideals are patterns by which we endeavor to shape

[1] See Mark 14:36

our lives. We must understand the meaning of "The Oneness" and merge our physical and mental ideals with the spiritual ideal of the soul. Our spiritual pattern should not be trimmed to fit us, but we should grow to fit the pattern, whose Maker and Finisher is God.

The True Ideal

The true ideal is the highest spiritual attainment to be reached on this material plane; hence, it follows that our ideal must be found in Christ, who is the Way. He that climbs up some other way is a thief and a robber to himself. All real seekers after truth recognize this, although they may have different ways of expressing it. The following quotations will illustrate this.

"To think, to speak, to act from the consciousness of my divine self that I may be like Him, that I may do the things He said I could do, and help those who have not heard His voice—this is my ideal."

"Thou glorious One, radiant beyond finite mind, I would manifest Thee more fully. Thou tender and loving Father, for Thy Son's sake give me the testimony of the Spirit to bear witness with my spirit that I am a son of God, and likewise help me fully to realize that my brother is one with Thee. Awaken me to the newness of life, peace, love, knowledge, and understanding—then I shall be reaching my true ideal."

"My ideal is spiritual in essence, regardless of where it leads. Christ the Guide, Christ the Leader, and Christ the Way. His ways are my ways, and His ambitions are my ambitions. To be Christlike is my ideal. We are the sons of God and should act as such."

"My ideal is to be a perfect channel through which the will of the Father may be done, whether in the physical, the mental, or the spiritual plane, and to return to the Father from whence I came. My hopes and desires are in the One by whom all were created."

In Jesus we have the way, in Him we have the example, and in Him we have all the attributes of the Ideal manifested. His teachings and life of service to His fellow man show us the way we too must tread in attaining the height He reached. When in our relationship to our fellow man we are so perfected in the Christ Consciousness that each word, thought, and deed bring blessings to those we contact, then we may be sure that our ideal is the true one.

Attaining the Ideal

The ideal cannot be man-made, but must be of the spiritual nature that has its foundation in Truth, in God. Know the first principle:

> The gift of God to man is an individual soul, which may be one with Him, and that may know itself to be one with Him and yet individual in itself, with the attributes of the Whole, yet not the Whole.   *262-11*

Such must be the concept, or the ideal, whether of the imaginative, the mental, the physical, or the spiritual body of man. All may attain to such an ideal, yet never become the Ideal, but be one with the Ideal.

With this ideal once set, there will be no fear. There will come to each of us that grace to dare to be a Daniel, to dare to stand alone. We attain our ideal by seeing the Father in others. Let our prayer be,

> God, be merciful to me! Help Thou my unbelief! Let me see in Him that Thou would have me see in my fellow man. Let me see in my brother that I see in Him whom I worship.   *262-11*

We reach this vision through Christ. It takes the penetrating light of His Spirit to discern the divine spark in fallen humanity. It takes the mind of Christ to bless and not condemn, to love and not censure. The fields are now ripe unto harvest, but the laborers are few. We must work, work, for the night of unbelief and doubt comes.

It is our heritage to catch the true concept of the Divine in all and to be, in truth, co-workers with God. As there is raised in ourselves more and more of the Christ Consciousness, we become free indeed, and with freedom comes the awakening—the awakening to the realization of the Ideal.

As we see others as the Christ sees them and strive to

consecrate ourselves to Him, then our daily acts, our words, and our thoughts will bring that understanding and realization of the Ideal manifested in us as well as in others. Let us look for good in everyone, speaking neither evil, harsh, nor unkind words to any at any time.

Let us do all that we know to do, in love, and leave the results with God. Let us hold fast to that which we have purposed in our inner selves, knowing that no emergency in a material way or manner may arise that cannot find its solution in spiritual inspiration, for His promises are sure. Offenses may arise, yet with each and every fear there is that from within which will quiet our troubled minds, even as He quelled the tempest on the sea. As we seek, we find; as we knock, we are heard. If we are timid, fearful, or overcautious in giving out the hope which has sustained us, then we grow more weak and fearful ourselves.

Conclusion

Have we chosen the spiritual Ideal? Are the things in our own lives measured by that Ideal? When we sincerely examine ourselves and know that our standard is what we see in the other fellow and come to realize that our God is manifesting in and through him, we know that the Ideal we are setting for ourselves is one that will lift us up and cause us to be merciful, even as our heavenly Father is merciful. Then we may be assured of the peace that passes understanding.

What is our Ideal? The Christ-Way. Let us not be anxious, but wait on the Lord, knowing that He is faithful who promised, "If any man hear my voice, and open the door, I will come in to him, and will sup with him, and he with me."[2]

[2]Rev. 3:20

Lesson IV

FAITH

"Above all, taking the shield of faith, wherewith ye shall be able to quench all the fiery darts of the wicked."

Ephesians 6:16

Affirmation

Create in me a pure heart, O God. Open Thou my heart to the faith Thou hast implanted in all that seek Thy face. Help Thou mine unbelief in my God, in my neighbor, in myself. *262-13*

IV

FAITH

[Based on Edgar Cayce readings 262-13 through 262-17]

What Is Faith?

Faith is an attribute of the soul. It is the inner spiritual knowledge of the Creative Forces of the universe. As we become cognizant of the physical body through the senses, so we may become aware of the soul through the activity of its attributes. Faith may be denied or renounced until it ceases to exist within the consciousness of the physical mind. It can be acknowledged and exercised until it will remove mountains. That which is brought into consciousness through the activity of spiritual forces, manifesting in and through the spiritual force of the individual, becomes the essence of faith itself. Hence, it has been termed by many that faith, pure faith, accepts or rejects without basis of reason, beyond the ken and scope of that which is perceived through—that which man brings to his activity through—the five senses.

"Faith," as defined by Barnabas, "is the substance of things hoped for, the evidence of things not seen."[1] Faith knows that it has already received and acts accordingly, doubting nothing. It is the builder of the seemingly impossible. It is that which has brought into manifestation all that has ever existed. God is, faith is. It is the evidence of God's promise fulfilled. Man's divine privilege is to accept, use, develop, and enjoy the fruits of faith.

In the material world we often mistake confidence for

[1]P.R. See Hebrews 11:1

faith. We are prone to depend upon our physical senses, forgetting that they are deceptive. This is not faith, but confidence—for confidence comes through the physical senses. When trials and disasters arise, that are seemingly beyond our power to control, we begin to sink, and immediately in hopelessness and distress we cry out, "Lord, help me, I perish!" It is then that the Voice speaks, "O ye of little faith!"[2]

Let us examine ourselves and see whether we are holding to faith or confidence. We must view spiritual things from spiritual standpoints and accept them in a spiritual way.

Many say, "We have faith," but they begin to explain that it applies to mental and not to material things. We say, "We believe, but—" which means there is doubt, the very opposite of faith. Remember, when we entered this material plane, we became subject to material laws. It is the failure of our senses to perceive and fully to understand these laws that brings many of us to the point where we have little real faith.

There is a world before us to be understood: the mysteries of the universe, the law of love, the power of thought, and the matchless gift of faith. We stumble, we falter, even when we have the divine promise, "If ye have faith as a grain of mustard seed, ye shall say unto this mountain, Remove hence to yonder place; and it shall remove; and nothing shall be impossible unto you."[3] With such a promise, should we not cry out, "Lord, I believe; help Thou mine unbelief"?[4]

Need of Faith

Faith is victory, for where there is faith rightly placed, there is no failure, but true success. "Be thou faithful unto death, and I will give thee a crown of life";[5] that is, be full of faith and have as a reward life's crowning glories. We know that all our development, physical, mental, and spiritual, depends upon our faith in God, in our fellow man, and in ourselves. Just in proportion to the amount of faith we place in God and in ourselves, just so great is our development. Why not take God at His word, letting

[2]Luke 12:28   [3]Matt. 17:20   [4]Mark 9:24   [5]Rev. 2:10

our faith become a living faith by acting in the manner that shows to the world that we know ourselves to be sons of God. There is no other way to real victory.

Let us have more faith in our fellow man. We may not agree with him, but who knows whether he is not more in line with the divine plan than if he were following our lead? It is well to remember that our Ideal is manifested through our fellow man as well as through ourselves, and it is, therefore, more necessary for us to trust him, even though appearances may be against it.

It is not only our privilege, but our duty to have faith in ourselves. We are workers together with God, and when we doubt ourselves, we doubt the God within us. He has promised, "I will never leave thee, nor forsake thee."[6] Call to mind the words: "I can do all things through Christ which strengtheneth me."[7] In His Name we are more than conquerors. It is only by having the faith of a little child in the abiding presence of the Christ that we can hope to inherit the kingdom.

Faith is a bridge that spans the gulf from the seen to the unseen. It is often all we have left when everything seems against us. With this in mind, how diligently should we cultivate and seek to increase our faith when all is going well with us, in order that it may be a strong fortress when the storms of life begin to beat upon us. Lord, increase our faith!

How Faith Is Developed

Faith is developed by the use of it. It cannot be taught or forced, neither can true faith be destroyed. Through the exercising of faith, we are able to give enlightenment to others.

Let the mind be in us that was in Jesus the Christ; then there will come faith that is sufficient unto every need, even that faith which removes mountains, changes the destiny of nations, yea, and even brings worlds into existence. Do we believe this? Then, how may this be accomplished? By opening our hearts in meditation to the unseen forces that surround the throne of grace, beauty, and might, and at the same time by throwing

[6]Hebrews 13:5   [7]Phil. 4:13

about us the protection found in the thought of the Christ, we can accomplish this. (See 262-3.) Then let us add to our faith works which show forth attributes that are expressions of His Spirit in the world. Thus shall our faith develop and become to us evidence of things not seen. We must show by our actions in our daily lives that we believe, that we have faith, and that we know as we use what we have, more will be given.

In times of trial, let us think of the faith that has sustained others in troubles far greater than ours. When our conscious minds would magnify our doubts, let us awaken our faith by rising above the cries of the flesh. Are we not children of the Most High? Let us hold steadfastly to this gift that is God-given, that will lead us upward along the way of life.

In studying and applying cooperation, in using the knowledge we have gained in knowing ourselves, in holding to our ideal, and in never letting our faith falter, we are building step by step that which may become living truth in the lives of individuals with whom we come in contact. As we apply what we know, there is given a greater understanding of how our faith may increase and become a living thing in our experience. We are in our daily lives reflections of what we worship. Let our light so shine that others seeing the light in us may glorify God.

Where Faith Abounds

Only into the heart that is free from selfish love can there come a faith that will sustain in all conditions of life. Our faith must be a sustaining faith, a living faith, one that we can try out daily and know to be sure and steadfast. Where there is real faith, there is no fear, for with faith in the abiding love of the Father, what cause is there for us to have an anxious moment?

Every step of the way is shown to us who are faithful, for His word is a lamp to our feet. When the way is dark and barriers seem impassable, then the light of the Sun of righteousness[8] shines forth to us who abide in the promises He made.

[8]See Mal. 4:2

When faith abides within, we have true freedom and
the assurance that we have no master save Jesus the
Christ, and that we are protected by the strong arm of the
Father. The feeling of security, protection and peace that
passes understanding is found nowhere else. Faith is the
promise sent on before to show that whatever we ask we
have.

Self-Analysis Necessary

The solution of mental problems is more important to
man than physical, although this does not seem true to
the average man lost in the twisted paths of materialism.
Free the mind and the battle is almost won. Mental
anguish is far greater than physical, for the mind can
conquer physical pain, but it is necessary for the spiritual
forces to aid the suffering mind.

The savage worships a god who will send rain and sun-
shine and protect him from lightning. The philosopher
seeks a god who will give him peace in mind and soul. Do
we know in whom we believe? If so, then the ideal or
standard toward which we move becomes the basis for
the activity of faith in constant action from the mental,
imaginative and spiritual forces. Thus we may express or
bring into manifestation that which is held as our ideal—
not for self-exaltation, but rather to show the blessings
we have received and to see them manifested in the lives
of others.

Let us look within ourselves and know that we are
workers together with God. We should analyze ourselves
to find out just where the flesh is weak, where we are most
likely to fail, and then seek a constant reinforcement of
spirit that will make us hold on with unwavering faith to
our Ideal.

Evidences of Faith

"When the day is dark and the way is obscure and we
can still hold on, there is evidence that there is faith.
When the sea of life is rough and we have the courage to
step out boldly on the troubled waters, it is because there
is still the divine gift at the very center of our being that is

saying, 'Peace, be still,'[9] for 'I am with thee and will not leave thee.'[10] We have heard it. We can hear it always, if we will only take the time to listen."

"When doubts arise and the clouds of despair are thick, do we not call out in the night, 'My God, my God, why hast thou forsaken me?'[11] Does not an answer come? Are we not stronger by having an experience that gives us a better understanding of our brother who suffers in the same manner?"

"Some years ago, I was with a party that was visiting a noted cavern. Everyone seemed very happy. After being in the cavern for a short time, I became very much frightened. The thought came to me, 'How terrible, how dreadful it would be, if we could not find our way out!' The very air seemed to press in upon me. Ages seemed to pass. Then came the Voice that has sustained me so often: 'Lo, I am with you always.'[12] 'Be not afraid.'[13] With these words there came the strengthening of my faith."

"When loved ones are lingering in pain and no earthly help is nigh, are there not evidences of the faith of our fathers revived, when we pray and receive help? It brings the greatest comfort to us, not only in the trying times but at all times, to know inwardly that His promises are sure."

Reward of Faith

Our rewards are in proportion to the faith we exercise. "According to your faith be it with you."[14] "Whatsoever ye shall ask in prayer, believing, ye shall receive."[15] There is no limit to the reward. It is ours to measure, and ours to claim. "Prove me...if I will not open you the windows of heaven and pour you out a blessing, that there shall not be room enough to receive it."[16]

Let us open ourselves as channels, and have complete faith in God, for the battle is the Lord's. It remains to be seen what we can do when we give ourselves unreservedly into the hands of the Father. "And I will pray the Father and He shall give you another comforter, even the Spirit of Truth, who will guide you into all Truth."[17]

[9]Mark 4:39   [10]P.R.   [11]Mark 15:34   [12]See Matt. 28:20   [13]John 6:20
[14]Matt. 9:29   [15]Matt. 21:22   [16]Mal. 3:10   [17]P.R. See John 14:16; 16:13

"And what shall I more say? For the time would fail me to tell of Gedeon, and of Barak, and of Samson, and of Jephthae; of David also and Samuel and of the prophets; who through faith subdued kingdoms, wrought righteousness, obtained promises...And these all, having obtained a good report through faith, received not the promise: God having provided some better thing for us, that they without us should not be made perfect. Wherefore seeing we also are compassed about with so great a cloud of witnesses, let us lay aside every weight, and the sin which doth so easily beset us, and let us run with patience the race that is set before us, looking unto Jesus, the author and finisher of our faith."[18]

[18]Hebrews 11:32-33, 39-40; 12:1, 2

Lesson V

VIRTUE AND UNDERSTANDING

"Finally, brethren, whatsoever things are true, whatsoever things are honest, whatsoever things are just, whatsoever things are pure, whatsoever things are lovely, whatsoever things are of good report; if there be any virtue, and if there be any praise, think on these things." Philippians 4:8

Affirmation

Let virtue and understanding be in me, for my defense is in Thee, O Lord, my Redeemer; for Thou hearest the prayer of the upright in heart.   *262-17, A-14*

V

VIRTUE AND UNDERSTANDING

[Based on Edgar Cayce readings 262-18 through 262-20]

Introduction

In defining virtue and understanding, we must remember that these words are used here in their fuller meaning as expressions or activities of the soul or spirit forces, not as mental or emotional concepts. To establish a common ground, let us say that to be true to that which is pure in our purposes is virtue. Virtue is full cooperation that prepares the way for enlightening and uplifting humanity. Virtue is keeping ourselves in tune with Creative Force, enabling us to know ourselves as we are known by others. Virtue is holding steadfastly to the Ideal that is set in Him, the Lord of Lords and King of Kings. Virtue is pureness of heart, pureness of soul, and pureness of mind that come through His Spirit bearing witness with our spirit. Virtue is the seasoning of faith, the essence of hope, and the crowning element of truth—an attribute of God.

True understanding is beyond the reason of the senses. It is the power to experience and interpret the laws that govern the expression of Creative Force, or God, in and through the physical, mental, and spiritual bodies of mankind. Where there is virtue there will be understanding, for one follows the other. Understanding is the reward of virtue. With virtue, therefore, comes understanding, for the two are as the tenon and the mortise; they fit one with the other. Knowledge is not always

understanding. Daily, many experience miracles of
which they have no understanding. Few that have mere
knowledge get understanding. An understanding of the
mysteries of life comes to those only who make a close
approach to the Throne. We may know the course of the
stars, the intricate formulae of mathematics, and the
secrets of sciences, but we cannot understand God's
laws until we have experienced that closeness with the
Divine that makes us realize that we are part of His laws,
rather than mere observers of them. It was no miracle to
those who understood Stephen when he said, "Behold, I
see the heavens opened, and the Son of Man standing on
the right hand of God."[1] It was no miracle to the Master
when He fed the five thousand with five loaves and two
fishes, for He understood the law of supply. It requires an
understanding of God's law (love), when such a message
is heard even today as, "Lo, I am present with you in this
room—I have chosen you as ye have chosen me. Keep the
way thou knowest, keep the path thou hast trod, for He is
able to deliver thee in every trial, and unto him that is
faithful comes the crown of life. As I am lifted up in thy
consciousness, so will I be lifted up in the consciousness
of others."[2] With such an understanding comes a finer
and more sincere relationship with others, and a higher
spiritual concept of self. We link virtue and understanding because they are expressions of the activities of
the soul forces. Virtue built into the mind is the only sure
path to true understanding. Knowledge assists when it is
in harmony and in accord with the Ideal; otherwise, it
may become a barrier, a curse, and a dark pit from which
it is hard to escape.

Virtue and Understanding Are Spiritual

Those of us who seek virtue and understanding must
walk with God. We never sink so low that we do not at
some time feel a longing to look up, and to seek something higher than our own selfish desires. Often it takes
only a song, a kind word, or a friendly deed to cause the
fire of hope to leap and such a prayer to be uttered as
"Lord, be merciful to me a sinner!"

[1]Acts 7:56   [2]P.R.

We may be counted worthy to point out the way only after we have walked the way with Him, who was tempted in all ways like unto us, yet without sin.

If our hearts are open to the consciousness that comes from abiding in Him, there will be no misunderstandings, for the power of the Holy Spirit will awaken in each of us that which was ours in the beginning. The desire for virtue and understanding is already within. Spirit cries to spirit, "Purify me, cleanse me! Give me back my first estate, my virtue, my understanding, my God!" "As the hart panteth after the water brooks, so panteth my soul after Thee, O God."[3]

May our aspirations be expressed in the following words:

> O Thou divine and celestial spark, alive in some, dormant in others—Virtue, Understanding, Creative Force, God—have Thy own way in our hearts and lives, we pray!

Virtue and Understanding Are Essential to Right Living

Both virtue and understanding are essential to right living, or righteous living. They are needed in meeting the daily problems of life that arise within us as well as in our relationships with others. We sincerely desire that our standards be correct, but none of us can choose aright unless we are guided by the Holy Spirit. It is hard to know the original cause or the final result of a decision influencing another. We may not know what trial or tribulation may have caused a brother to err. If we know, it is because we have ourselves experienced some similar tribulation. It is then that our standards are measured by Him who abides within our holy temple, and they fit perfectly with the Ideal within our less fortunate brother. We have no cause to find fault or condemn.

Virtue and understanding are the requisites for spiritual work. What we do not possess we cannot give. What we do not live we cannot teach others to live. Unless we are pure, how can we expect others to be pure? Our very words and acts condemn us. We must be and

[3]Psalm 42:1

know before we can direct, or before we can rightly guide others who are seeking the safe harbor.

There is a desire in each of us to live better day by day. We wish to reach a certain goal. If we are choosing the highest, the best, we will not be satisfied with anything less. It is well for us to remember that the highest goal is not reached at a single bound, but step by step—here a little, there a little. It is encouraging to know that no good deed is lost, not even a good intention; but all are built within our very souls and will bear fruits, some thirty, some fifty and some a hundredfold. It is by deeds, righteous deeds, that we rise. "We climb to heaven leaning on the arm of a brother whom we have helped." (See 281-4.)

The Way to Virtue and Understanding

The way to virtue and understanding is through prayer and meditation. The approach to all understanding must come from a proper concept of our needs in the physical, the mental, and the spiritual phases of our lives. This is the approach of the Master Jesus.

Others may point the way, but have they the virtue and understanding of Him who said, "I am the way, the truth, and the life"?[4] He proclaimed no way except the one He, Himself, had trod. He so lived the way that He could say, "Follow me."[5] The way is open to all.

We are moving along the path when we begin to see ourselves as others see us, when no unkind thought of our brother is allowed to lodge in our hearts, and when we seek earnestly to be pure in heart, pure in mind, pure in body, and pure in soul.

The way is straight and narrow, so narrow that we must have no will but the Father's, that we must have no purpose but to do His work, and that we must have no aim but to reach the Christ Consciousness. This leads to virtue and understanding. "Seek, and ye shall find; knock, and it shall be opened unto you."[6]

Personal Experiences

"I have found the way. It is through divine love, and it

4John 14:6   5P.R. See John 21:22   6Luke 11:9

is for all who desire it. I prayed seven years for divine love. It is a living thing within me, giving me strength to love those who have wronged me, giving me the sight to see good in those who would do evil. It is in me the healing power. I give thanks that I now recognize the God within me who is helping me to express divine qualities."

If we would have virtue, then let us step out on faith—faith in the purity of self, faith in the perfection of our brother, and faith in the promises of God. Virtue is the reward of faith, and understanding is the reward of virtue. Through faith the veil is lifted and we can go within ourselves, within the holy of holies and be transformed into the image and likeness of the Son of God.

"I did not feel I had the necessary virtue for an upright life. After much thought and meditation, the words came to me, 'Faith is the chief cornerstone.' This helped me, for I knew that I could exercise faith. I then began to give thanks that I, through faith in the Christ, had virtue, a cleansing of body, soul, and spirit. Understanding came to me."

We must have implicit faith in God and in His promises, if we would have the cleansing power of His Spirit manifesting in our lives. We must have full faith in our brother, if we hope to be as pure as we demand him to be. We must have more faith in ourselves and in the power of the Spirit ever ready to manifest in and through us, if we expect to do our greatest work. Unless we have faith, how can we expect to see the glories of God? He that doubts is condemned. It is only through faith that we are justified, for belief in God is counted unto us for righteousness.

Virtue Is a Defense, Understanding Is a Weapon

Virtue has the dynamic power of the Holy Spirit. It strengthens the spiritual quality of man and engenders a greater knowledge of the Maker and a greater faith in Him. The more we open our hearts as a channel of blessings to others, the more power we possess. Keeping the channel clear, open, and ready to be used, we see the

seemingly impossible begin to take place and we come to
realize that no weapon that is formed against us shall
prosper. Happy are we when protected by the impreg-
nable defense found in the same pureness of ourselves
that we demand of others.

Virtue is a defense against all temptation to censure,
condemn, or criticize—for with it we see with eyes that
are looking for the pure. We see behind the vice of other
souls, made in the image of their Maker. We feel that they
need our love and our help along the way. With virtue
within, we never retard the development of others.

As with virtue comes understanding, so with understanding comes divine light. Understanding is a strong
and tried weapon whose blade is never bent. It has ever
been a weapon in the endless warfare for truth. When
once the enemy is conquered, he is at the same time won
as an ally, for he stands in awe in the presence of a power
that gives an understanding of his real intents and purposes. Only with virtue and understanding can we rise
above the tumult in the battle of life, and, with the
Master, pass through the midst of it and go our way. How
simple when we understand! How wonderful when we
are pure in heart, pure in mind, and pure in spirit!

The Effects of Virtue and Understanding
on Ourselves and Others

Virtue and understanding have to do primarily with
ourselves and with our relationship to the Creative
Forces. They are reflected in our judgment of others, for
our conduct is a reflection of our inner thoughts. To think
nobly is to act nobly. It is a privilege to think, provided we
think with a mind that is in tune with the ideal that is set
in the Christ. We may compare the daily building of
ourselves, mentally, physically, and spiritually, to the
construction of a house. Are we choosing those attributes
that will help our development? Are we casting aside the
imperfect stones, using only the good? Are we placing
them evenly in line? Are we ready to be passed on by the
divine Inspector? If we can answer these questions in the
affirmative, then we are hastening our development

toward God. The quality of the structure depends upon us and upon us only. We are building for ourselves either hovels or holy temples.

No man liveth to himself. How we live, act, and think not only is reflected in ourselves but also has its effect upon others. As we put into practice love, mercy, justice, patience, and forgiveness, others catch the same spirit. This is illustrated by one who came in contact with those who had received spiritual cleansing. "They made me better," she said, "gave me back my living faith, instilled in me a desire to realize—that God lives and is speaking through men. They gave me hope and new interest in life. Before I met them my worship was form; afterwards it became more spiritual and I began to reach out for the joy that seemed to be theirs."

Finally, we know we have passed from death unto life because we love. We know that new life now courses through us, and that a new and strange peace is ours that makes us in accord with divine will. What we once despised now we cherish, and the world we formerly cherished now ceases to attract. We give thanks to God for this unspeakable gift of spiritual understanding which is now ours through the cleansing power of the Holy Spirit.

May the following words be ever upon our lips:

> Let virtue and understanding be in me, for my defense is in Thee, O Lord, my Redeemer; for Thou hearest the prayer of the upright in heart. *262-17, A-14*

Lesson VI

FELLOWSHIP

"If we walk in the light, as He is in the light, we have fellowship one with another."   I John 1:7

Affirmation

How excellent is Thy name in the earth, O Lord! Would I have fellowship with Thee, I must show brotherly love to my fellow man. Though I come in humbleness and have aught against my brother, my prayer, my meditation, does not rise to Thee. Help Thou my efforts in my approach to Thee. *262-21*

VI

FELLOWSHIP

[Based on Edgar Cayce readings 262-21 through 262-23]

Introduction

In preparation for the task before us, let us become more conscious of the divine Spirit within, that we may go on. May we face the issues before us as those called for a purpose. May we rely on His promises, for while we are often weak and selfish—and the work is great—He will encourage our spirits, our hearts, with the presence of His Holy Spirit, so that there may be no idleness or delay in us.

A spark of the Divine that is forever seeking its source is within each of us. As we develop our spiritual forces, our soul forces within, we fan this spark into a flame which brings realization of our oneness and fellowship with the Creator of all things. There is a longing in our hearts for this fellowship—an urge driving us hither and thither in search of happiness and satisfaction, onward in search of God.

In the beginning, all knew a perfect fellowship with the Father, and in the knowledge and understanding of this fellowship men walked and talked with God. Again, this same fellowship is offered to all, a promise of the Father, through the Son. It is the reflection of this fellowship which expresses itself in our love for our fellow man, whom we innately feel to be one with us as part of the all-inclusive Whole. As we manifest love toward our brother, we increase or awaken our consciousness to a more complete fellowship with the Father, and we more fully realize that He moves within others as He moves within us. The brotherhood of man is but a shadow of fellowship with the Father. It is a true expression of the fellowship that exists in spirit.

Am I My Brother's Keeper?

Thousands of years ago there arose a question in man's heart, "Am I my brother's keeper?"[1] It is still being asked. Until this is fully answered in our hearts in God's way and put into practice in our lives, we cannot hope to have the fellowship that is our rightful heritage. When we fail to reach "the mark of the high calling" that is realized in service, we endeavor to justify ourselves by making the old inquiry, only to receive the answer, "The voice of thy brother's blood crieth unto me from the ground."[2] No wonder we are miserable and cast down, and have fears that paralyze our efforts. Is it not because we know in our hearts that sin lies at our door?

"Behold, what manner of love the Father hath bestowed upon us, that we should be called the sons of God."[3] God gives only love to His children and pities them even as an earthly father pities his children. It is only when we sever relationship from divine Love by failing to suffer with our fellow man, to bear his burdens, and to forgive him that we are out of harmony and sympathy with all that makes life worth living—fellowship with the Father. Have we not at some time realized this?

If we would be in a position to commune with the Spirit within and if we would seek to know His face, then let us be kind and gentle, compassionate and loving to others less fortunate. Manifesting love for our brother is manifesting love for God, in whom "we live and move and have our being."[4]

We are enjoined not merely to ignore the shortcomings of our brother, but to love him in spite of his shortcomings and to show such faith in the power of the Spirit within him that he will catch our vision and in time come to realize his strength and seek to rise to higher planes of

[1]Genesis 4:9   [2]Genesis 4:10   [3]I John 3:1   [4]P.R. See Acts 17:28

consciousness. We need not flatter him or lead him to overestimate his strength; rather we should help him to understand himself and to know that he has a friend who will stand by in time of need—one who will extend a hand if he is about to fall into temptation. This answers the whole duty of man to man, of brother to brother, and of man to his Maker, for "Inasmuch as ye have done it unto one of the least of these my brethren, ye have done it unto me."[5]

The test is this: Are we willing to deal with others as we wish them to deal with us? May we ever be bound together in service to others through the fellowship which we have in Him.

Our Fellowship with God

If we wish to know how we stand with God, let us examine ourselves and see how we feel toward our neighbor. This companionship that we are seeking with God is found in the friendliness we show our brother. It is evident that our actions, our words, and our thoughts indicate too plainly our failure to seek fellowship with the Father. Let us examine ourselves that we may know what is buried in our hearts and minds that may be blinding us or binding us; and if we have anything against our brother, let us pray for forgiveness, knowing that His mercy is sufficient for all.

Seek God where He may be found, even in the heart of a neighbor. How well do we know God? Just as well as we seek to know and understand our fellow man, and just as well as we seek to magnify the divine consciousness in him. Do we seek far for the Divine in this direction? Do we not judge our brother from appearances rather than by righteous judgment? Do we not often overlook the motive which may have prompted his misconduct? Do we realize that deep down in the heart of our brother there lies buried a celestial fire that burns ever before the altar of our God? Then let us seek him out and, in spite of the rebuffs that we may receive, love him, not for what he appears to be, but for what he really is—not because he is human and needs our sympathy, but because within him

[5] Matt. 25:40

there is the Divine that merits our adoration.

What is more beautiful than fellowship! The Master sought it, that He might do the works of God. He did not withdraw from men, but mingled with them, sharing their sorrows, living their lives, and relieving their sufferings. We cannot hope to emulate His example, however, unless we abide in the Spirit that gives the strength. "I am the vine, ye are the branches. He that abideth in me, and I in him, the same bringeth forth much fruit; for without me ye can do nothing."[6] The Master taught that love and service go hand in hand. What greater love could He have shown than to lay down His life in service for His fellow man; yet that is just how far the Master went to demonstrate His power over sin, death, and the grave, that those who seek life might know the way. May the Spirit help us to be willing to serve, and to see in our neighbor his higher self at all times, in all places, and under all circumstances.

If we would have fellowship, we must rely on His promises and keep His commandments, which are not grievous. The greatest commandment "that ye love one another," He called a new commandment, and it is still new to many of His followers.

We affirm that we want to know God, but do we really mean it? If we are really sincere, will we not be eager to sacrifice our desires, our opinions, and our whims, that the wonders found in the knowledge and understanding of the works of the Creator, our God and Father, may be revealed to us? May we not be willing to endure, that we may be counted worthy to share in the glory to be revealed to those who have given themselves wholly to His service? How easy the way when self is lost in Him! How easy to follow when we have been told to use what we have and more will be given.

Let us remember the Master's words to Simon: "Feed my sheep."[7] None of us can approach the Father with any degree of assurance when we feel and know in our hearts that we are out of harmony with ourselves or others. We are out of harmony with ourselves when we lack faith in ourselves, or when we minimize the power of

[6]John 15:5   [7]P.R. See John 21:16

the God within and forget that all power in heaven and earth is committed to our keeping—if we will attune ourselves to the Infinite Source of that power. We are out of harmony with others when we think of them as less divine than ourselves or as possessing less divine power, love, and mercy. Therefore, it is necessary to begin with ourselves to purge our hearts and minds and to become more conscious of the divine Spirit within others. This is necessary if we hope to have the fellowship with the Father that will cause us to realize our oneness with Him.

Prayer and meditation are the essential factors that will keep alive within us this perfect harmony. Are we seeking this fellowship? Would we have God draw nigh unto us? If so, then let us draw nigh unto God, approaching often the Throne of Grace, with mercy in our hearts.

"The heart is deceitful above all things, and desperately wicked,"[8] that is, the unregenerated heart, the heart that knows not the cleansing of the Spirit or the awakening of the presence of God. Let us search our hearts. "If our heart condemn us, God is greater than our heart, and knoweth all things."[9] He knows our joys and sorrows; He knows how we have tried and, therefore, in spite of our failures, shows love and mercy. If our hearts condemn us not, then we have faith in God, faith that He will keep His promises.

Let us be ever ready to forgive. This is the way that God deals with us. He has pardoned our sins and blotted out our transgressions. How much more should we be willing to forgive others! If the thoughts, deeds, or acts of others have caused us pain, let them not be magnified in our own mind or charged to their account. Let us who have pledged our loyalty bear the cross, since we have the promise of the crown. Let us help our fellow man by our patience and forbearance and show him that love is a living thing. What great love hath the Father bestowed upon us that we might show forth His glory among men!

Let us strive to be kind, training ourselves to be considerate of those who do not seem to appreciate it. Yes, be kind when it is the hardest. It is worth the trial, not for the reward we may expect from others, but because we

8Jer. 17:9   9I John 3:20

cannot allow anything to mar the fellowship we would have with the Father. One unkind word may not leave a lifelong pang in the heart of another, but it will place us so out of harmony with all that we count worthwhile that its effects will follow us perhaps through many years. Great kindness may be shown through little deeds. He who gives a word of comfort to the disheartened will have his reward. Though this is a small service, it may help as nothing else would help. Let us not count any good act lost. No seed falls to the ground without the Father's knowledge. It was only a cup of water to the tired Master at the well that set the occasion which brought many out of the city seeking to know more about the water of life. May we lose no opportunity to bind up the broken-hearted, to pour oil on the troubled waters, or to heed the command, "Comfort ye, comfort ye my people, saith your God."[10]

Let us remember that we shall give account for every idle thought; therefore, let us think on those things that make for brotherly love. As we develop step by step, here a little, there a little, we learn cooperation, we get better acquainted with ourselves, trust more fully in our Ideal, have our faith strengthened, gain virtue and under-standing, and more and more become aware of our fellowship with the Father and our duty to others.

Fellowship with God, the Need of the World

The crying need among men of all ages has been that man must understand himself, his relationship to his neighbor and to his Maker, and know that they are in-separable. These are one. It is impossible to separate God from His creations, for He manifests through them.

It is impossible to love God and hate our brothers, whose souls are made in the image and likeness of God. Love and hate cannot live in the same heart. Too many of us count fellowship unimportant. Many of us are selfish and are neglecting to let those attributes that reflect fellowship have a place in our lives. If we are making this mistake, we know it, our brother knows it, and more than all, the Father knows it. The world is poorer because of

[10]Isaiah 40:1

the stumbling blocks we have put in the way of others. In this we are not only blocking our own development but also the very purposes for which we were created.

This fellowship with God, of which the world is so much in need, does not simply embrace kindness and gentleness toward friends but also includes love for enemies. This relationship to God will likewise make us see that to love our enemies does not mean simply to have the right attitude toward them, but rather to have in our hearts a yearning for them to know the Way. In their most terrible acts we can see a power for good misdirected. This attitude will help the world to better understand the obstacles and trials of others, including other nations, since peace on earth and good will toward men must first be experienced by the individual before it may be realized among nations.

With this knowledge of the need of fellowship, how can we hold a spirit of revenge, dislike, or judgment? Would we dare to bind others by our thoughts?

Love and brotherhood, reflections of fellowship with the Father, instilled into the hearts and lives of all, would bring this world into such a happy state that th. millennium would be here in deed and in truth. It will be well for us to examine ourselves in order to know whether we as individuals are doing our full part. Are we fulfilling the law of love toward rich and poor, high and low, saint and sinner, friend and foe?

There is no better place to practice brotherly love than in the home. Just watch its effects upon members of the family. If at home we cannot answer kindly, it will be better not to answer at all. It is far better for an angry thought to die unexpressed than for it to kill the good in the life of the speaker and retard the development of the one to whom it is addressed.

Duty of Those Who Have Fellowship with the Father

"Ye have not chosen me, but I have chosen you."[11] In fellowship there comes a duty to others. There are certain bonds to be kept, and certain laws to be understood and

[11]John 15:16

reverenced. "Who shall stand in his holy place? He that hath clean hands, and a pure heart"[12]—such have fellowship with the Father. They delight in His laws and understand and cherish them.

Yet many of us may complain that the way is hard and that the obligations are many and heavy to bear. Are we not judged out of our own mouths? Should we not rather take Him at His word and know the truth of His assurance, "My yoke is easy, and my burden is light,"[13] and that He will place no burden upon us that we are not able to bear?

One who sought true fellowship told of the experience in these words: "I saw a vision. In it I was able to discover what it meant to be selfish. I beheld myself in the school of life, using what little spiritual food I had for my own benefit. I was sitting on the side of a hill, eating. I soon realized that the ground upon which I was sitting was beginning to crumble. My food was also rapidly diminishing. A voice said, 'To him that hath not, it shall be taken away from him even that he seemeth to have.'[14] Suddenly, I became aware of my destitute position. My food was gone, the earth was receding, and great billows of water were about to overtake me. I arose and began to climb upward, slowly, laboriously. I eagerly sought and accepted help from those I had formerly considered on lower spiritual planes than I. These words came to me: 'Whatsoever a man soweth, that shall he also reap,'[15] and, 'All things whatsoever ye would that men should do to you, do ye even so to them.' "[16]

That which we think, we become. That which we are, we reflect. That which we reflect, others judge us to be. We may be mistaken in our estimation of ourselves and others may misjudge us, but God looks on the heart and knows all things. He knows our purposes and what we are capable of becoming. The Master said, "Thou art Peter, and upon this rock I will build my church,"[17] though He knew that Peter in his weakness would deny Him. It is our duty to walk before men in such a manner that they may see the good within us and thus glorify the Father. It is our duty to be on our guard at all times, lest

[12]Psalm 24:3, 4   [13]Matt. 11:30   [14]P.R. See Luke 8:18   [15]Gal. 6:7
[16]Matt. 7:12   [17]Matt. 16:18

we lose courage when called into the "judgment hall" to give a reason for the faith that is in us. We must see that our fellowship is able to stand the test in every trial so that no one can point the finger of scorn at us and say, "Hypocrite, even your words condemn you!" It is our duty, yea, our privilege, "To make all men see what is the fellowship of the mystery, which from the beginning of the world hath been hid in God,"[18] and now is being revealed.

Fellowship Brings a Peace
That Passes Understanding

As we have dealt with our fellow man, we may expect to be dealt with. What cause have we for fear if we have obeyed the Voice? We have become as little children putting our trust in the Giver of all good and perfect gifts, and we know that He will reward us according to His goodness and mercy. "Great peace have they which love Thy law; and nothing shall offend them."[19]

To whom do we look for this peace? Who hath brought the Pleiades into being, or set the bands of Orion, or the waters of the deep that are cast upon the land, or brings breath into the life of all His creatures and supplies the union with those Creative Forces that makes for the songs of the spheres? The Lord is His name. Under the shadow of His wing there is peace and no cause for fear. (See 262-23.)

Let nothing stand between us and the Father, but rather let us cast aside the things that have hindered in the past and allow no care to weigh us down as we go forth in His name day by day. Do we not know and are we not confident that "All things work together for good to them that love God, to them who are the called according to his purpose"?[20] There may be things we do not understand now, but those things we can safely leave in the hands of the Father, knowing that He will reveal them in His own good time. Let no worry or condemnation enter our minds that might hinder the fellowship we have with the Father. The time is at hand. "He that is unjust, let him be unjust still; and he which is filthy, let him be

18Eph. 3:9   19Psalm 119:165   20Romans 8:28

filthy still; and he that is righteous, let him be righteous still; and he that is holy, let him be holy still."[21] It is not for us to judge, but to work, to serve, and to rely wholly on the promises: "Lo, I am with you alway, even unto the end of the world."[22] "Peace I leave with you, my peace I give unto you . . . Let not your heart be troubled, neither let it be afraid."[23]

Let our meditation and prayer be expressed in the following words:

> How excellent is Thy name in the earth, O Lord! Would I have fellowship with Thee, I must show brotherly love to my fellow man. Though I come in humbleness and have aught against my brother, my prayer, my meditation, does not rise to Thee. Help Thou my efforts in my approach to Thee.   *262-21*

[21]Rev. 22:11   [22]Matt. 28:20   [23]John 14:27

Lesson VII

PATIENCE

"In your patience possess ye your souls." Luke 21:19

Affirmation

How gracious is Thy presence in the earth, O Lord! Be Thou the guide, that we with patience may run the race which is set before us, looking to Thee, the Author, the Giver of light.   *262-24*

VII

PATIENCE

[Based on Edgar Cayce readings 262-24 through 262-26]

Introduction

God is the God of patience. All nature declares this. It is written in the rocks, the caverns, the hills, and the valleys—yea, deep in the heart of the earth. It is no less written in the souls of men by Him who has shown Himself to be long-suffering, forbearing, and willing, though it takes ages, for all to come to the knowledge of the light.

Patience is an activity of the God-mind within each soul. Its expression involves mental, physical, and spiritual thought and action. Through patience we learn to know self, to measure and test our ideals, to use faith, and to seek understanding through virtue. Thus all spiritual attributes are embraced in patience.

As we exercise patience day by day, we know how well we have put into activity the lessons learned from past experiences. Patience puts all the virtues into action. With patience we become channels of blessings to others —serving not in our way, but in His way—not once, but as long as there is need of service.

Value of Patience

Patience is a test of our development. Manifested in our daily lives, it shows whether we have used or abused the opportunities presented during former experiences.

What great understanding results when we exercise this attribute!

It is through patience that we get a better understanding of the Father and His relationship to His children. It is through patience that we get a better understanding of the crosses that we bear day by day.

He that is without crosses has ceased to be of notice and is no longer among the sons. We may be called upon to bear not only our own crosses but those of others. If we would approach the Throne, we must come leaning upon the arm of a brother we have helped. This manifests our relationship to each other.

Patience, as nothing else, shows growth. We often find ourselves so able to meet some difficult problems that we feel we have solved them before. Doubtless we have, again and again. At other times we are not able to cope with problems not nearly so intricate. Why do we have such experiences? If we fail in meeting these in the right spirit and find ourselves beaten, do we not act the parts of weaklings? As we realize our mistakes, we become ashamed that we lost hold of ourselves, and resolve that we will profit by the mistakes. Because of these experiences, we should ever afterwards count ourselves happy to endure, and be more willing to wait until we are better understood, and until we can better understand. It is the lessons learned through patience that in the end strengthen and help us; then we become examples to others. Something, too, has taken place within us, for something is written that the hand of time cannot efface. We have found a pearl of great price to be set in the soul, where it will remain through all eternity!

How kind is the wise provision of the Father! He gives to us each moment just what we are able to use. We cannot use aright that which we do not understand. "I have yet many things to say unto you, but ye cannot bear them now."[1] As we do our bit to make His promises real by showing our brother that we understand his burdens and are ready to help him bear them, we become more and more able to know the love of the Father and more conscious of our own growth.

[1]John 16:12

The beauty of the soul shows in the life of an individual who has patience. This comes to those who have a constant, prayerful attitude for a purposeful life. In order to have this beauty of the soul's expression, it is necessary that we forget ourselves. It is not altogether an outward growth but an inward one, too. It is the result of introspection, which is the foundation of deep meditation. Love is manifested in every word and act, even as it was in those of the Master. So, through patience let us magnify His attributes in our experiences. There is nothing to regret in exercising patience—there is everything, in the loss of it. We are building for eternity. Results do not always manifest at once.

One individual relates the following experience: "I was called upon to pass through a great trial. My supply of patience and endurance seemed to become more and more depleted as the days went by. Beginning to realize, at last, that I was only an instrument—a channel through which God's will was being manifested—my strength and courage gradually returned until, without fear, I faced the issues at stake and came to a clearer and better understanding of the problem. It was worth all to have patiently waited and to have felt His presence."

His presence with peace is the promise to us who with patience endure the crosses that are set before us day by day.

Means Through Which Patience Is Gained

In patience we become aware of our presence before the Throne. Let us seek often, then, to awaken our inner selves. With patience this may be accomplished. If we lose hold on ourselves, through the lack of patience, there is the opportunity for the entering in of those things that would make us afraid. In waiting we have the promise that His strength is sufficient for us. There is no danger of defeat, and there is no cause for fear. It is necessary, however, that we be in perfect attunement with our ideal, if we are desirous of possessing this virtue, patience, that is so necessary for our spiritual growth. There may come many harassing experiences that would seem to separate us from the Maker, but each experience has its reward. As we seek, let us know that the Comforter, who will come to us at all times, is near, and we will never be left alone.

The understanding of His laws will come, little by little, as we apply what we already know. The development of patience requires prayer and a constant watch upon ourselves, lest we be off guard and let slip an angry word or a quick retort, causing someone to stumble. Think on these things. Selfishness retards our progress in gaining patience. The recognition of this means the taking of a bold step, but a necessary one, if we would have that patience with others that we are desiring for ourselves. Lose self in Him; find self in service. Lose self in Him; find self one with the Father. The step is magic, the realization divine, when every act, every thought, and every word is so actuated by the spirit of patience that others will endeavor to emulate our example. This becomes the natural experience to the heart that recognizes God in everyone.

In the trials that arise day by day, our patience is tested. We begin to grow as we overcome and put behind us each new obstacle. Passive submission will not suffice; our patience must be an active, growing force which rises to meet each new trial. Whom the Lord loveth He chasteneth and purgeth every one, for corruption may not inherit eternal life, but must be burned up. Let us know that our God is a consuming fire and must purge everyone that would be one with Him.[2]

We overcome only through patience. We develop by pressing on, by expending spiritual energy, and in so doing we open the way for God to lend the sustaining strength of His presence in times of trial and tests that come to all.

How may we more perfectly live the life that we may through patience gain the better understanding? By applying what we know day by day. The Spirit does not call on us to live what we do not already know and understand. In doing there comes the knowledge and the understanding for the next step. When should we begin? Today, for "Now is the accepted time,"[3] we read. Let us

[2]See Hebrews 12:6; I Cor. 15:50; Deut. 4:24   [3]II Cor. 6:2

enter in through faith and with patience wait for the next step. Those of us who make ourselves unworthy of being tried are unworthy of being trusted for the entering in.

It Takes Patience to Run the Race

The trying of our faith worketh patience,[4] we are told in Scripture. Day by day, step by step, the race is run. When we think our patience is entirely exhausted, then we have lost patience with ourselves. What a hell it becomes if we become impatient with ourselves! How quickly we must hasten to analyze ourselves and make the necessary corrections and adjustments! Influences from within are stronger than from without; thus our higher selves stand ready to help, if we are really anxious to set ourselves right. What an opportunity for growth and a closer approach to Him! Let us live just today, as if the race were ended, the work completed—as if upon this day's endeavors depended the fulfillment of all of His promises. If we expected the Master, the Christ, to dine with us today, what would we have to offer as the fruits of our lives, our thoughts, our acts, or our deeds?

Patience is a virtue that has no vacation. How watchful we must be, lest malice or censure creep in, and we lose everything for which we have striven! We are called upon at all times to lay aside those things that hinder, and to run with patience the race set before us. The race must be run, for it is the way back to the Father. Let us be thankful that we do not have to run alone. "I am the way . . . no man cometh unto the Father, but by me."[5] Only the activity of patience, with trust in Him, will enable us to meet all trying conditions and rise above each new barrier.

Personal Experiences

"When I have gained an understanding of true cooperation necessary for each activity and have lost sight of self in service, then I have the knowledge of His presence abiding within, and more and more I express patience—the patience that feeds my soul. I can walk and work and wait peacefully in Spirit and know all is well!"

[4]See James 1:3 [5]John 14:6

Patience is the chief cornerstone of soul development. It is, moreover, the watch set at the gateway leading from the physical body to the soul. With it we not only meet the weaknesses of ourselves, but are able to estimate the strength found in developing various attributes of the soul—love, faith, and hope. What we are, what we have been, and what we intend to be are shown more in the patience we exhibit than through any other virtue. It shows just how we have stood the tests in the past: how we have met and conquered them, or gone down in defeat before them. Patience shows just what our development is: whether we are ready to bear with others and overlook their shortcomings, or are primitive in thinking that our way is the only way to truth and real understanding.

"In your patience possess ye your souls!"[6] "For what shall it profit a man, if he shall gain the whole world, and lose his own soul? Or what shall a man give in exchange for his soul?"[7] When we possess this priceless gift, received from the hands of the Father, shall we, in order to assert our rights, pay so high a price that we would give our soul in exchange for self-aggrandizement?

There may be much to bear before we can have the title to the possession cleared in our minds, but through patience in each trial we become stronger for the next. The Master was asked, "How oft shall my brother sin against me and I forgive him—till seven times?"[8] The reply was, "I say not . . . until seven times, but until seventy times seven!" Is seventy times seven built within us? Are we ready to bear and forbear until the end, or ready to give insult for insult, blow for blow? Are we not, by our lack of self-control, showing only how far we are failing to measure up to the standard we have set for others? Much is buried deep within these souls of ours, much that we should know. As we more and more exercise patience and put into practice what we know, we will grow in grace, knowledge, and understanding. Lord, direct us in the patience of the Christ!

As we understand more perfectly what it means to be a channel of blessings to others and become more aware of the presence of the Father, greater patience will find a

[6]Luke 21:19   [7]Mark 8:36, 37   [8]Matt. 18:21

place in our lives.

"Be patient; stablish your hearts, for the coming of the Lord draweth nigh,"[9] we are instructed. When? This is the time—today. The time draws nigh for each of us to become more aware of the necessity of magnifying His presence through the patience we have with our fellow man, in order that He may be glorified in us through the promise of the Father. For "Inasmuch as ye have done it unto the least of these, my little ones, ye have done it unto Me."[10]

Then let our prayer be expressed in these words:

How gracious is Thy presence in the earth, O Lord! Be Thou the guide, that we with patience may run the race which is set before us, looking to Thee, the Author, the Giver of light.   *262-24*

---

[9]P.R. See James 5:8   [10]P.R. See Matt. 25:40, 45

Lesson VIII

THE OPEN DOOR

"Behold, I stand at the door, and knock; if any man hear my voice, and open the door, I will come in to him, and will sup with him, and he with me."   Revelation 3:20

Affirmation

As the Father knoweth me, so may I know the Father, through the Christ Spirit, the door to the kingdom of the Father. Show Thou me the way.   *262-27*

VIII

THE OPEN DOOR

[Based on Edgar Cayce readings 262-27 through 262-30]

Why shrinkest thou, my soul?
Doth thou not know new strength comes but by faith
And faith renewed, and effort newly made?
And couldst thou even dare to hope to catch
The faintest glimpse of the Ineffable,
If thou doth not stretch out to thy full length
The helping hand to open wide the door?
[By Mrs. 2118 for this lesson]

Introduction

The kingdom of God, the glory of the oneness in the Infinite, is the eternal destiny of every soul, the ultimate goal of every entity, regardless of his place or position in the seemingly complex scheme of things. In each there is felt that urge to press on. Through ignorance and misunderstanding many seek only the gratification of selfish desires, fighting, struggling, as it were, against the inflexible laws which an all-wise Creator has set. Eventually, each struggling soul must face the realities of life and make his will one with that of the divine Maker. With this comes peace in the realization of "I and my Father are one."[1]

The door to the kingdom of the Father is through the life, the Spirit of the life, manifested in the Christ Consciousness in the material world. It is opened only by the efforts of an individual. Throughout the previous lessons, continual emphasis has been placed upon the awakening of the Christ Consciousness. Each lesson

[1]John 10:30

has presented some attribute of the soul, some faculty of the inner self, which, if magnified in the conscious activities of the individual day by day, will add to and strengthen the growth of the soul's expression through the physical man. May we not ask these questions? Who, then, of us has learned to be truly cooperative one with another? Who has learned himself sufficiently to know wherein he stands in relation to his fellow man? Who has set the ideal wholly in Him? Who has magnified the faith in the Father and in the Son, that it may be accounted to him for righteousness? Who has virtue and understanding? Who has fellowship with the Father? Who has in patience possessed his own soul?

The Christ Spirit comes as a result of Christ-like action. To each it comes as a realization of the activity of the soul forces. As the creative urge stirs the seed of the flower, just so the activity of the soul expressed through cooperation, a knowledge of self, the ideal set in Him, faith, virtue, understanding, and patience stirs an individual, and there is upward growth. As the flower in due time blossoms forth, just so the soul of man, through the Christ Spirit, comes into its full power and glory.

The Preparation of Self

The preparation for the way is a preparation of self. Each of us is the door that He, the Way, may enter. "Behold, I stand at the door, and knock."[2] "I am the way, the truth, and the life."[3] We must work to bring that consciousness, that awareness of His presence, into our material and mental affairs of life. The lesson must ever be, the spirit is the life, the mind is the builder, and the physical is the result.

Only when we completely surrender to the working of the Christ Spirit, can we say truthfully the door to the kingdom within is open. All selfish thoughts must be obliterated and replaced with the desire to be used by Him in carrying out His will in the world. When we seek our brother's good, rather than our own, we may expect our reward in proportion to the good we send out. When we become self-centered, we eventually feel that we are

[2]Rev. 3:20   [3]John 14:6

being cheated in life. It is then that we close ourselves to the good we might give out, and at the same time, build a barrier to the good that might flow to us.

As we seek to know the way, we must come in single-ness of purpose and think not of the hindrances that are man-made; rather, know in whom we have believed and recognize that He has brought all things into being. As we seek and know this, we are His. In choosing Him, He has chosen us. As we realize we are one with Him, we become workers, pointing others to that joy, peace, and happiness that we have found. Will we not be faithful to the calling wherein He has called us?

How shall we begin? Let us take that which we have in hand, that which we have builded day by day, and, without fear, open the door that He may enter in and abide with us. Faith is the beacon that lights the path to the open door of the Father's house. Service is the password that admits us into the banquet hall. Come ye blessed of my Father, enter into the Kingdom prepared for you—for as ye have done unto one of the least of these, My brethren, so ye did it unto Me.[4]

We have to contend with many conflicting forces when we would have faith and serve others. Selfishness and sensitiveness shut the Ideal from view and prevent a wholehearted cooperation with our fellow men in our daily lives. They may so retard our development that nothing seems worthwhile. These hindering qualities can even bring thoughts of self-destruction. It is only when self is put aside and the Spirit is allowed to lead that we indeed are free and able to accomplish anything that is of real, lasting value. When the thoughts of doubt, lack, and self-condemnation begin to creep in, the door begins to close more and more, until not even a ray of light may filter through to light the way. When these thoughts are allowed to remain in control, there is no despair more terrible. We are shutting out the light and living behind closed doors—closed to God and His goodness. Do we wonder, that where these thoughts are uppermost there are suicides, murders, and sins of every kind in evidence? Are not many in the world at this time

[4]See Matt. 25:40

ready to be shown a more perfect way? We show through service that as He overcame the world and became the Way, just so may we, who follow in His steps, overcome all things.

How to Open the Door

We must open the door if we would have the Christ enter. As we, with the Christ Consciousness as the standard, manifest His love in our daily walks in and before men, so we open the door. Then it is that we heed the call to the Spirit within that stands ever ready to commune with us. It does not come in the whirlwind, but as a still, small Voice. If we listen and trust, it will teach us all things and bring all things to our remembrance.

If we would recognize this great Intelligence, this great I AM that knocks for admission into every heart, then let us heed these words: "Ye that have named the Name, make known in thy daily walks, in thy acts, the lessons that have been builded in meditation and prayer."[5]

A good king will continually seek a contact with his subjects that he may understand their needs, and he will be quick to reward any special obedience to the laws. How much greater will the Heavenly Father, who watches over His children, be ready to help them! Yet, God requires that we seek His face and believe that He is, before He reveals Himself. We must make the effort, if we wish to open the door to His Kingdom. "If ye will be my people, I will be your God."[6]

What is the way to the Father? It is through the Christ (having the Christ Consciousness) that we come to the Father, open the door, see the way, and hear His voice. When we close our ears to the pleadings of the less fortunate, we close the door to His presence; for in so doing we do not manifest the mind of the Christ. "When saw we Thee naked and clothed Thee, hungry and fed Thee, a stranger and took Thee in? Inasmuch as ye did it unto one of the least of these little ones, ye did it unto Me."[7] Let us know that when we speak a kind word or lighten the care of a brother, we open the door that He may enter, and through Him is the way into the Father's

[5]P.R.   [6]P.R. See Hebrews 8:10; Lev. 26:12; Jer. 30:22
[7]P.R. See Matt. 25:38, 40

Kingdom, and there is no other.

As we seek to magnify His Spirit, let us know that we, too, become doors through which others may be drawn into the way. We are living in a material world of three dimensions; the spirituality that we wish to reflect must be expressed in and through material thought and activity, if we sincerely desire to reach and to awaken others. What is to be gained if we shout from the house-top concerning brotherly love and forget the little acts of kindness or the smiles that will lighten others day by day?

When we are aware of the Christ Consciousness within, we begin to put into action the Christ Spirit without. It is only in the application of our spiritual attributes day by day that we become living examples, showing our at-onement with Him; thus, we not only open the door, but as channels, are doors. Let us not forget, as we work, that those we meet along the way are seekers also and are the Israel of the Lord.

How to Know the Father

As the Father knoweth us, so we may know the Father. The Father judges us in our relationships to our fellow men. As we give, so we receive; as we measure, so it is meted to us; as we forgive, so we are forgiven—not because the Father wills it, but because we have chosen it to be so by our own acts, words, and deeds. It is the Father's good pleasure to give to each nothing less than the kingdom. Would we know the Father? Let us then stretch out our hands in love and sympathy to our faltering brothers, and as we lift them up, so shall we even then in that hour be lifted up. Acknowledge each in his respective sphere of development, for that is the necessary stage of his experience. Let us remember that Zaccheus climbed higher that he might have a broader vision, and on that day dined with Truth.

We know the Father by exemplifying His attributes in the earth. Let us not hope to reach all in a day, but little by little, line upon line, precept upon precept, here a little, there a little, until we come daily to know more and more of the Father.

As we lose ourselves in Him, earnestly desiring to put into practice the prayer, "Not my will, but Thine, O Lord, be done in and through me,"[8] we realize our oneness with the Christ, the door to the kingdom of the Father. We will find that the Father is not an arbitrary master, one who is demanding our service, but an all-wise Provider, a Father who understands all our needs. This was understood by the Psalmist when he sang, "O how I love thy law! It is my meditation all the day."[9] We will get a new concept of the Father the moment we make His will our own.

The Great Need for Service

We are our brother's keeper. A new revelation is taking place. A new order of things is being born. Old things are passing away and, behold, new things are about to appear. Man is considering his relationship to his fellow man as never before. Let us catch more clearly the note of compassion and love taught by our Elder Brother and, in His Spirit, pass it on. Let us not sit and wait until tomorrow, but use that opportunity, that privilege, and that promise today. Let selfishness be swallowed up in selflessness.

There is a great need for service. A stream that has no outlet becomes stagnant and impure. Self-development is not the whole purpose of service. There is a greater need. We must see to it that our brother, too, comes to the knowledge of the Light. There are responsibilities as well as joys in service. Storms may come, but it is He who stills the tempest for us. He brings rest to those who are tired. No matter what the trials may be, keep the faith. Let self be as naught that He, the Guide and Leader, may be better understood by those who look to our activities. He is the Light, and as we walk closer to Him the way becomes brighter.

If we would be channels, we must demonstrate in our lives what we teach. Let us choose each day some truth, live it first for self, then for others, that they may see our good works as we put into practical operation just what

[8]Mark 14:36   [9]See Psalm 119:97

we say we believe and teach. It will work. The Master said, "Lo, I am with you alway, even unto the end of the world."[10]

The Kingdom of the Father

To be aware of the Christ Consciousness within is to open the way for the Christ Spirit to manifest in our lives. The way is open to all who seek. The trials may be many, but through the Christ Spirit we are able to meet them. There is a consciousness of His force, power, and activity upon which we may draw. When doubts arise, it is a call to prayer. Let no doubt linger, but give thanks that it is only a look onward and upward that will again restore the faith upon which our hope is built.

The possession of an earthly kingdom is worth the seeking of a lifetime. There is not only responsibility but honor in its possession. There is a certain satisfaction that something is being accomplished by self and, perhaps, for others. How much greater is a possession in the kingdom of the Father—that kingdom prepared for us from the foundation of the world. What can stand in our way? Only self! As we realize this, may we not push self aside and let the Spirit lead us fully into that possession which is our birthright, and thereby exercise the benediction of Him who said, "All power is given unto me in heaven and in earth"?[11]

> Be still, my children! Bow thine heads that the Lord of the Way may make known unto you that have been chosen for a service in this period when there is the need of that Spirit being made manifest in the earth, that the way may be known to those that seek the Light! For the glory of the Father will be made manifest through you that are faithful unto the calling wherein ye have been called! Ye that have named the Name make known in thy daily walks of life, in the little acts of the lessons that have been builded into your own experience, through those associations of self in meditation and prayer, that His way may be known among men. For He calls on all—whosoever will may come—and He stands at the door of your own conscience, that ye may be aware that the Scepter has not departed from Israel, nor have His ways been in vain:

[10]Matt. 28:20   [11]Matt. 28:18

For today, will ye harken, the way is open—I, Michael, call on thee!   *262-27*

Bow thine heads, O ye sons of men, would ye know the Way: For I, Michael, the Lord of the Way, would warn ye that thou standest not in the way of thy brother nor sittest in the seats of the scornful, but rather make known that love, that glory, that power in His Name, that none be afraid: for I, Michael, have spoken!   *262-28*

Hark! O ye children of men! Bow thine heads, ye sons of men: For the glory of the Lord is thine, will ye be faithful to the trust that is put in each of you!

Know in whom ye have believed! Know that He is Lord of all, and His word faileth not to them that are faithful, day by day: for I, Michael, would protect those that seek to know His face!   *262-29*

Let our prayer be expressed in these words:

As the Father knoweth me, so may I know the Father, through the Christ Spirit, the door to the kingdom of the Father. Show Thou me the way.

262-27

Lesson IX

IN HIS PRESENCE

"And I will walk among you, and will be your God, and ye shall be my people."   Leviticus 26:12

Affirmation

Our Father who art in heaven, may Thy kingdom come in earth through Thy presence in me, that the light of Thy word may shine unto those that I meet day by day. May Thy presence in my brother be such that I may glorify Thee. May I so conduct my own life that others may know Thy presence abides with me, and thus glorify Thee. *262-30, A-12*

IX

IN HIS PRESENCE

[Based on Edgar Cayce readings 262-31 through 262-34]

"Lift up your heads, O ye gates;
And be ye lift up, ye everlasting doors,
And the King of glory shall come in."[1]

Introduction

Our thoughts, our words, our activities, and our general outlook on life are motivated by our concept of Him whom we worship. Our inner life and reaction to all environs and associations are expressions of what we have done about or with the knowledge and consciousness of His presence abiding with us.

When we keep His presence as a thing apart, something to be experienced or something of which to be aware, then, when we are disturbed in some manner, we lose sight of the fact that to abide in His presence can be the experience, the knowledge, and the understanding of all who seek to do His bidding. His presence abides with us always, for it is in Him we live and move and have our being. We must realize this, and come to know and understand that we are sons of God.

God is Spirit, standing back of everything in creation. God is One. We cannot separate Him from His creation. We may try to do so, but in so doing we become dual, mystified, and confused. When we separate ourselves or think ourselves apart from our Maker, we are like ships without rudders.

The oneness is ever existent, but it is only through our

[1]Psalm 24:7

realization and our acknowledgment of its existence that the change is worked in us, and life takes on a new aspect. We are free-will agents. God is not a person in the sense that we think of persons; yet, to those of us who seek His presence, He is very personal. He is God to all—Father, to those who seek.

It is our oneness with the Father that the Master stressed while on earth in a physical body, when He declared that He could do nothing of Himself: It was the Father within Him that did the works. Just so we, to do the works of God, must seek ever to be conscious of the Presence within. All the guidance, help, supply, joy, peace, and whatever goes to make life worth living is within. "Seek, and ye shall find; knock, and it shall be opened unto you."[2]

Know, O ye children of men, the Lord thy God is One. Each spirit, each manifestation—either in this or any other sphere of development—moves toward the knowledge, the understanding, and the conception of that One—Him, God, Jehovah, Yah—the All One.

It is only when we listen to the still small voice within and know that His presence is with us that we come to the realization that we are one with Him.

The Knowledge of His Presence

It is within the human soul, the simplest unit of God (which man would make complex), that we will find Him abiding. Sensing the presence of God within and without, we become quiet, throw off anxiety, and are conscious of a renewing power. The Spirit of God speaks through the soul—the soul forces. How may we know this? We must study and meditate until we realize what attitude we hold concerning His presence. Men of old have said, "Such knowledge is too wonderful for me; it is high, I cannot attain unto it."[3] We, too, may feel at times that it is physically impossible to attain to that knowledge. May we not take God at His word and accept His free gift of grace, love, and mercy? "If any of you lack wisdom, let him ask of God, that giveth to all men liberally, and upbraideth not."[4] "I am the Lord. I change

[2]Luke 11:9   [3]Psalm 139:6   [4]James 1:5

not."[5]

We obscure the knowledge of His presence by considering it as a thing apart. Let us not quench the spirit within. As His spirit bears witness with our spirit, not only will we understand ourselves better, but there will come a fuller understanding of our brother, our friend, or our enemy. As we go fearlessly on into whatever work is before us, let us trust in His care, knowing that His presence will overshadow us. The Light will shine ahead and show the way. He will keep our stumbling feet from faltering and will allow no harm to overtake us. May we live each moment aware of His presence and let our work testify for us.

As self is less and less magnified and more hope and reliance is sought in His Word, each of us will become more and more aware of His abiding presence. All who would know Him must believe that He is, and that He is a rewarder of those who diligently seek Him. How often have we read, "The Lord is my shepherd,"[6] and doubted the truth of it as applying to us. By submitting our will to divine guidance we come step by step into the realization that He will withhold no good thing from those who seek Him, who seek to do His will.

The Preparation of Self

The realization that we are ever in His presence is not always easy when we allow the cares of the world to creep in and draw us away in body and mind. As we are in various stages of growth, so we are in different states of consciousness. What might be absolutely necessary for the preparation of self for one of us, for another might be secondary. It is well, however, for all to observe:

1. The laws of righteous judgment and clean living.
2. Special hours for meditation and prayer, that we may be strengthened during times of severe temptation and trials.
3. The realization that He is ever with us, whether we are in sorrow or joy; for mind is the builder.
4. Such standards of conduct that others may know that what we profess with our lips to believe is in keeping with that which we hold as our ideal.

[5]Mal. 3:6   [6]Psalm 23:1

We should be living examples of what we profess. Many of us follow from afar and our actions are not in keeping with the Christ Consciousness. We often give others the wrong impression of His attributes manifesting through us.

"If ye love me, keep my commandments."[7] What are His commandments? "Inasmuch as ye have done it unto one of the least of these my little ones, ye have done it unto me."[8] "I will come again, and receive you unto myself; that where I am [in consciousness], there ye may be also."[9]

Finally, as we abide in His presence, though there may come trials of every kind, and though tears may flow from the breaking up of the carnal forces within, the spirit is made glad, even as He in the hour of trial smiled upon him by whom He was denied.

Let us remember that physically, mentally, and spiritually we continually reflect our understanding of His presence. Let us study to show ourselves approved unto Him day by day; for in so doing the light of His presence shows forth in our precepts, in our examples, in our words, and in our works.

As we look upon our fellow man, we find that his activities, in whatever sphere he may be, are expressions of the attitudes he has builded regarding God. His life reflects what he worships. His actions show the spirit which is within him. Is he not using the same measure for us?

In the physical body, good health is a reflection of our observance of physical laws. Even the small details involving the care of the body are important, for they are either in accord with laws that bring a finer type of expression or lead to inharmony. The physical surroundings, the type of companions sought, and every physical action express to others our concept of how near God, law, and love are to us.

As the activities of the body reflect the strength of the physical man, so the activities of the mind reflect the strength of the mental body. The question of controlling our actions physically is in part answered by man-made laws and customs; but the problems of controlling our

[7]John 14:15   [8]P.R. See Matt. 25:40   [9]John 14:3

thoughts, which truly may be just as harmful and out of tune with the Infinite, are personal matters which must be met by each individual. Thought vibrations go out, words are spoken, deeds are done, and all carry to others their influences and their impressions of our understanding of God.

How spiritual are our lives? How often do we seek through meditation and prayer contacts with our Creator? Do our attitudes and our philosophies of life center about a spiritual ideal? Others look for these signs and are influenced by them. We believe, but do we express our belief in our words, thoughts, deeds, and attitudes?

Experiencing the Abiding Presence

The consciousness that He walks and talks with us, and that His promises are ever present, brings abiding peace. This makes for joy in service, even though it requires that there be greater and greater sacrifices of the carnal forces within our experiences. Joy does not come through service that benefits self. He that serves through kind words, thoughts, or deeds, gives of himself, even as He, the Master.

With the realization of being in His presence comes that peace which casts out all fear and loneliness. There comes a feeling of being a part of the scheme of things. This is recognizing the God within as well as without. With this realization the way is easier. We will have more consideration for others. Condemnation will be cast aside and we will have a desire to bless.

"My presence shall go with thee, and I will give thee rest."[10] The protection of the Holy Spirit is His promise, if we are faithful. As we use what we know, not waiting for physical results before going on to the next step, we will find—when we least expect it—that which we desire has been granted. We are children in faith, knowledge, and understanding; we have to be taught and disciplined. Could a child be trusted with a live wire? No more could we be trusted with divine power until we, through love, discipline, and faith come to understand the divine law. It is the Father's good pleasure to give us the kingdom. It

[10]Exodus 33:14

is ours only when we learn through patience to possess
our souls.

Personal Experiences

"I was arrested on a false charge. In the presence of
hardened officers of the law these words came to me: 'If
God be with you, who can be against you?'[11] And then
came the words of the Master, 'Be not afraid.'[12] His
presence was greater than any other, and the situation,
which had the material outlook of humiliation and
shame, was turned to the glorifying of His name in the
earth. My awareness of the great need of His presence
made me more conscious of it. In Him we do, indeed, live
and move and have our being. Each thought, word, and
act is an opportunity to advertise His presence. Let us
then be an advertisement for God."

"I was asked to give a talk in public. The request came
so suddenly that I had no opportunity to prepare myself.
I was tempted to devote my period for meditation to study
the subject, but the Spirit forbade, assuring me He that is
within is greater than he that is without. I harkened and
with scarcely a thought appeared before the con-
gregation. Never had I felt so keenly the presence of
the Spirit as on this occasion. The words came without
effort. I felt that there was a message of helpfulness,
inspiration, and power being given through me. It was
not I, but the Spirit within, that was doing the work.
Others bore witness that the message was to them one
above the ordinary, not only in words, but in power, and
in presentation. Surely, we are strong when we acknowledge our own weakness and rely on the Presence within.
It is only when we forget God that troubles overtake us. If
we today, at this time of testing, would place our hope of
deliverance in the hands of the Father instead of man, we
would not fail to come out more than conquerors."

"There is within me a knowledge that His presence
abides with me always as a part of me, not apart from me.
Through the toil of the day, through the quiet hours of the
night, He is always near. When burdens of the material

[11]Romans 8:31   [12]Mark 6:50

life are heavy, if I stop and listen, He assures me that He is with me."

Let Us Remember That Our Guard Is Ever in His Presence

Let us not be afraid in the presence of our Maker. He is willing to fulfill His promises to His children and ready to make known His ways unto those who will seek His face. The God who wrought the beauties of nature and set the laws which govern the harmonious symphony of the universe could not have left a part of His creation without guidance or without a sustaining force. The way is exemplified in the Son, and there are those universal Forces ever ready to aid and strengthen those who seek to travel this way.

> Bow thine heads, O ye men that would seek His presence. Be strong in His might. Falter not at thy own weak self. Know that thy Redeemer liveth and may this day make known in thy own heart His presence abiding with thee. Root from thy body, thy consciousness, aught that would hinder His entering in, for He would sup with thee. Wilt thou then, O man, make known thine own decisions? Will ye be one with Him? The way which I guard leads to that of glory in the might of the Lord. I, Michael, would guide thee. Do not disobey. Do not falter. Thou knowest the way.
>
> *262-33*

Let us glory in the Lord, not in self, and not in the wisdom of the earth—knowing that those who partake alone of the mental may easily become stumbling stones in the way of many. Let the Spirit of Truth that is within separate the chaff from the wheat, that we may enter into the full knowledge of His presence, and shut out those things that would hinder or cause doubt or in any way make us afraid. (See 262-32.)

Let this be our prayer:

> Our Father who art in heaven, may Thy kingdom come in earth through Thy presence in me, that the light of Thy word may shine unto those that I meet day by day. May Thy presence in my brother be such that I may glorify Thee. May I so conduct my own life that

others may know Thy presence abides with me, and thus glorify Thee.   *262-30, A-12*

Come! Let our hearts be lifted in praise and adoration of the wondrous love that the Father sheds upon the children of men.

Come! Let all be glad in the opportunities that are given to serve in His name day by day.

Come! Let us be joyful in the truth that "Inasmuch as ye did it unto the least of these my little ones, ye did it unto me."[13] Let the love of the Son be magnified in our lives that others may know that the joyousness of service brings peace and harmony to our hearts as we serve.

Come! Give thanks unto Him, for we would make our own lives and our own bodies a dwelling place of the love that the Father would manifest unto His children.

Come! Give place to His Holy Name that there may come joyousness in the hearts of men at the coming of the Christ into the lives and the experiences of many. (See 281-14.)

[13]Matt. 25:40

Lesson X

THE CROSS AND THE CROWN

"Fear none of those things which thou shalt suffer: Behold, the devil shall cast some of you into prison, that ye may be tried; and ye shall have tribulation ten days: Be thou faithful unto death, and I will give thee a crown of life."   Revelation 2:10

110

Affirmation

Our Father, our God, as we approach that that may give us a better insight of what He bore in the cross, what His glory may be in the crown, may Thy blessings—as promised through Him—be with us as we study together in His name.   *262-34*

X

THE CROSS AND THE CROWN

[Based on Edgar Cayce readings 262-34 through 262-38]

Introduction

"And ye shall know the truth,
and the truth shall make you free."[1]

If we come to understand these lessons and that to which they are leading, and if we hope to lead others in the way, we will find it necessary to analyze ourselves as to that which is, which has been, and which may be the impelling influence in our lives. We must discard everything that bespeaks selfishness or the magnifying of those desires that are gratifying only to the carnal influences in our lives.

In previous lessons, truths which could be applied in anyone's daily life have been presented. In studying this lesson, "The Cross and the Crown," we have the opportunity to take a definite stand, if we accept the following decision as our own: "For I determined not to know anything among you, save Jesus Christ, and him crucified."[2]

Do we feel that the cross represents something very definite in the life of each of us in our activities through the earth? The Christ Spirit has led in the presentation of truth in every age, in every clime, and came at last to the cross. He triumphed over death, hell, and the grave.

We choose this way not in an attitude of narrow-mindedness, but with a glimpse of the freedom which it brings—embodying, as it does, the light and truth of the

[1]John 8:32   [2]I Cor. 2:2

eternal and universal Spirit of the divine Creator.

Let us pause as we take up the study of this lesson and each ask himself this question: "Why have I chosen the way of the cross?" To troubled minds and tired hearts the way seems long and hard. Bypaths and shortcuts beckon invitingly, but the eternal self cannot be hushed for long with the things that satisfy not, for it urges ever onward toward the Everlasting. In passing through various experiences in the earth plane we come at last to recognize and accept His way, the way of service, the way of sacrifice, and the way of selflessness. We come to realize that there is no other way to attain our ultimate goal except the one trod by Him who made the supreme sacrifice that we might find our way back to the Father. We come to realize that, in fact, there is no other name given among men whereby we can be saved from self except through Him. The way of the cross which He chose will lead us out of our dissolution and into the light of understanding of our true purpose in the world; then the cross becomes a symbol of that which must be borne and overcome in every life. It is natural that as we study, the purpose of our trials becomes more apparent. We begin to realize that we must overcome if we would go on; those things in our hearts that hinder our progress must be torn out and cast aside. This is not easy to do without His help. He, having gone all the way, understands all our trials and temptations and, in love, willingly gives strength to us.

"I am the way, the truth, and the life."[3] In Him is all, and when accepted, the way is made so plain that we need not stumble. He is, indeed, the Light that lighteth every man. He came into the world understanding the laws of all things visible and invisible, and demonstrated His power over all forces, even death. He showed that the way is the way of love. As we emulate His example by taking up our cross daily, our desires are more and more to help others. We take upon ourselves joyfully the cares, the troubles, and the crosses of those whom we contact in our little world. It is, we know, because of this divine love, which is thus manifested in

[3]John 14:6

our lives, that we can rejoice in that we are counted worthy to choose the way of the cross and suffer for His name's sake.

With our Ideal, the Christ, as the pattern, we have the satisfaction that our approach to the Father is assured. We know that His Spirit is already bearing witness with our spirit, that we are heirs and joint heirs with Him. There is a consciousness of His force, His power, and His activity in every element of action.

So, in bearing our crosses we overcome those conditions that would hinder us in meeting the issues of life. When this is realized, the reason for choosing the way of the cross becomes evident. Not to choose is to acknowledge a misunderstanding of the purposes of life and the way toward the realization of life eternal. Who has learned obedience otherwise than through suffering?

Why Is It Necessary to Bear a Cross? Because One Was Borne by Another?

Our crosses are of our own making now, as well as in the beginning. The world was lost in the delusion of creative thought, seeking to reverse the process of God's law and find gratification in the lower forms of vibration. Thus we are confronted daily by crosses arising from our participation in the delusion of our senses. As we meet, again and again, the seeds we have sown, we come to realize that it is only through overcoming them that we can ever hope to reach again the estate from which we have fallen. Rebirth is the opportunity given to the sons of men by which this may be accomplished. Each life stands out, crowned with an opportunity to develop through overcoming, and it is only through selfishness or the gratification of the carnal nature that we lose. All have sinned and come short of the glory of God. The law must be met, either through the keeping of the law ourselves as under a taskmaster, or in the way provided through Him, who took upon Himself the burden of the world.

He overcame the world through experiences. In each experience He bore a cross, reaching the final cross with all power and all knowledge. He accepted the cross, hence doing away with that so-called karma that must be met by all. The immutable law of cause and effect is evidenced today in the material, the mental, and the spiritual world; but in overcoming the world, the law, He became the law. The law, then, becomes as the schoolmaster, or the school of training. We who have named the Name are no longer under the law as law, but under mercy as in Him—for in Him, and with the desires, there may be made the coordination of all things.

In bearing the cross, the flesh is crucified that His Spirit may be made manifest in the world. Each obstacle overcome adds strength for overcoming the next. We learn to overcome all that hinders us from becoming one with Him. This is made possible in service.

It is a glorious thing to know that we are helping Him through our service to others, to make known His purpose to bring mankind back to the Father. We never lose so long as we give. God gave His only begotten Son and received back a glorified Son who had shown a world the way back to the Father. It was the Son, in whom the Father was well pleased, who gave His all, even His life for His brethren. It is necessary that we bear the cross for our own development; but it is most glorious to have the opportunity to bear the cross for the sake of Him who made the way of escape possible for us.

Why Was It Necessary That He, the Maker of Heaven and Earth, Should Bear a Cross?

The God Force became ensnared in matter and, in the first Adam, fell. It was necessary, therefore, that the God Force, the Creator, individualize Himself as an example and by overcoming the world become the Law, in order that man might know the way out. So, in the last Adam all are made alive.

He, the Maker of heaven and earth, came to earth to bear the cross that He might add His experiences and activities to ours. His purpose was and is to lead the sons of men back to the realization that they are, indeed, sons of God and are at one with the Father.

In His bearing the cross, "It is finished,"[4] so far as the overcoming of the flesh and worldly things is concerned. He paved the way for His followers of every age. It was necessary that He, the Son of God, the Co-worker with the Creator, come to earth to demonstrate that the flesh could be overcome—thus giving glory to the Father who had made man for His glory. He bore the cross of materiality that He might change it to the glorified cross of spirituality. He left burning in the hearts of His followers the declaration, "And I, if I be lifted up . . . will draw all men unto me,"[5] and again, "He that believeth on me, the works that I do shall he do also; and greater works than these shall he do; because I go unto my Father."[6]

He went all the way. He was tempted in all ways, like unto us. He was numbered with the transgressors. "He was wounded for our transgressions . . . and with His stripes we are healed,"[7] and in all He was more than a conqueror. "Greater love hath no man than this, that a man lay down his life for his friends. Ye are my friends, if ye do whatsoever I command you. Henceforth I call you not servants; for the servant knoweth not what his Lord doeth: but I have called you friends; for all things that I have heard of my Father I have made known unto you. Ye have not chosen me, but I have chosen you."[8] What was the object of the cross? For what was the supreme sacrifice? That we through His strength might come to the knowledge and understanding of the way, might be able to overcome all things, and become kings and priests unto God.

Again, it was His way to show to mankind what divine love could do, and how it was possible to live a perfect, blameless life with all the disintegrating influences that surround us day by day. In every period of development through the ages, He has walked and talked with men. Those who understand know that whenever there was a need for man's awakening, the Son of Man entered the earth plane. The cross became the emblem of Him who offered Himself of Himself. For that cause, for that purpose came He into the world that He Himself, in over-

4John 19:30 5John 12:32 6John 14:12 7Isaiah 53:5 8John 15:13-16

coming the world, might gain the crown.

Why Did He Come into the World as a Man That He Might Bear a Cross?

It was through His thought and will that man took physical form. Only through the physical could the spiritual essence be aroused, awakened from its slumber, and set upon the path of spiritual progress. The question is answered: First, because of His own need to conquer the world in material manifestation, and second, because of the need of mankind for a guide, a teacher, and a saviour. The first is expressed in the following: "Though he were a Son, yet learned he obedience by the things which he suffered";[9] and the second is, "I am the way, the truth, and the life."[10]

He chose to take upon Himself the responsibility of overcoming the physical or making Himself the law through the fulfillment of all requirements. By adding His experiences and activities to ours He links man with God, bringing man in a closer attunement with God and causing him to become conscious of the Oneness of all. He came to show and teach us fellowship with God through our service to others.

As man, He knew the physical trials—doubts and fears, weaknesses and turmoils—of spiritual beings encased in material shells. He showed His ability as a man to demonstrate the possibility of man, as man, to bring spiritual harmony into physical vibration. He ever stressed the oneness of all force, demonstrating the direct relationship between man and the Creator. He came in the flesh to show that we in the flesh could become as He, God in Spirit; and taught that we may be one, even as He and the Father are one. Then this one, the Adam that first entered the world, must become the Saviour of the world. It was committed into His care. "Be thou fruitful, and multiply, and subdue the earth."[11]

Hence, the first Adam, the last Adam, was given power over the earth, and, as in each soul, the first to be conquered was self. Then all things, conditions, and elements are subject unto Him. So He became that One who

[9]Hebrews 5:8   [10]John 14:6   [11]See Genesis 1:28

was able to take the world, the earth, back to the source from whence it came. All power is given into His keeping in the earth which He has overcome. Self, death, and hell became subservient unto Him through the conquering of self. "In the beginning was the Word and the Word was with God, and the Word was God. The same was in the beginning with God."[12] The Word came and dwelt among men, the offspring of self in a material world. The Word overcame the world; hence the world became then as the servant of that One who overcame it.

Why Do We, as Individuals, Necessarily Bear Much That He Bore, and Yet Say That When Taking His Yoke upon Us the Cross Becomes Easy?

We must bear what He bore because we must travel the same way to perfection that He traveled. Along that way are experiences that all must have in order to gain the power and the knowledge of overcoming. As He took upon Himself the burden of the world, so we, in our own little world, must take upon ourselves the burdens of those about us. The yoke is easier because the burden is lighter. He bore it all. We bear only our part. In so doing we may become conscious of our real purpose to glorify the Creator and come to know that, after all, our crosses are only misunderstandings and misapplications of His laws. To practice, not preach, demands strength, power, and faith in the Ideal. Experience alone in overcoming can give a complete understanding of what it means for another to suffer, and yet not yield—to bear and forbear, and through it all love and forgive.

His yoke is easy because His presence abides with us, protecting us and sharing the burdens that otherwise would be too heavy for us to bear. Then, too, as we come to understand the meaning of our crosses and His abiding presence, our sufferings become lessons of wisdom, our turmoils more peaceful, and we rejoice as we find ourselves growing more and more into the likeness of Him who, by the way of the cross, became the Lord of lords and the King of kings.

His presence within is ever a bulwark of reserve power

[12]John 1:1-2

that enables us to resolve to acquit ourselves as men, to fight the battle, to win the race, and to wear the crown. (See Sam. 4:9.) Our Advocate with the Father keeps open the channel through which spiritual energy flows to us, so that we can make ourselves fit channels for passing on the truth to others. Spiritual understanding brings the knowledge that matter is the tool with which we may shape the nobler life into a likeness of the Creator. Harmony with His will, understanding, and application of His laws will bring at all times peace, not tumult; joy, not sorrow; love, not hate; and strength, not weakness. With His aid and the knowledge of His Spirit bearing witness with our spirit, the yoke that we are called upon to bear becomes, in fact, easy; and the burdens laid upon us are, indeed, light.

Does the Life Lived According to Our Own Faith, Our Own Understanding, and Our Own Walking in His Presence Explain Why Each Soul Must Bear a Cross?

As we seek to apply that learned in previous lessons dealing with attributes of the soul which should be magnified through our daily activities, we begin to realize our lack of application of those essential elements or attributes. We realize that we bear crosses because we have not yet learned to give complete expression to our soul faculties. We gradually realize how much of the inner self we have covered up, pushed aside for what we considered the more important desires of the conscious self. In so doing we have pushed ourselves further and further away from God. How well we begin to comprehend that our crosses are created by ourselves!

On the other hand, as we learn and apply these attributes of the soul, there comes joy and peace in the realization that the inner self is awakening and that it is ever on the alert to express itself through the exercising of faith, virtue, and understanding. Our relationships with others are made more perfect, and the ideal is set in Him. We see our crosses in a new light; we begin to catch a glimpse of the glory of the crown. We come to the realization of having, in truth, a part of the divine plan.

Why Has the Cross Been Chosen
Rather Than Some Other Philosophy
That Might Correlate the Material
and Spiritual Life?

The cross is the emblem of the subjective self of the One who bore the burden of the world. It is chosen, not because of the personality of the greater teacher, Jesus the man, but because of the way to the Father made plain through Jesus the Christ. It is the symbol of the life and teachings of Him who stirred the souls of men to express in all other forms of truth. It is a part of the truth of the world and the whole truth for those who choose its standard. It answers every question of the soul that is ready for light and satisfies the longing of the inner-most being. It is a symbol of the way of truth and light, universal in appeal, eternal and impelling, yet personal in application. In seeking the Divine, we have taken Jesus the Christ as our Ideal, for we find in Him the embodiment of all truth throughout the ages. Others may point the way. He said, "I am the way."[13]

Why Is the Cross, the Emblem of Shame,
Necessary for Those Who Seek the Crown?

We consider a cross an emblem of shame, for innately we realize it is symbolic of opposition to God's law. As in the beginning, the misuse of power given unto us brought suffering in this material world. The cross is the emblem of shame to those who in the material world judge from appearance. It calls for humility, not stub-bornness. It calls for suffering, not retorts. It calls for patience, not impetuosity. It calls for love of enemies, not hatred. It calls for forgiveness, not unforgiveness. All this must be borne in the cross that the crown may be laid upon the brow of the real heir, and not the usurper, who would never understand his subjects nor the road to true development. Who else has cleared the way for mankind and said to all, "Whosoever shall do the will of my

[13]John 14:6

Father which is in heaven, the same is my brother, and sister, and mother"?[14]

In bearing the cross we come to know the real meaning of the crown, the joy of completing a work, and the success that is the reward of a finished race. As we develop day by day, the idea of shame passes and there comes the joy of being one with Him in the great work of redeeming mankind. It is, indeed, an emblem of opportunity, and we come to see more and more the face of the Master reflected in each cross we bear.

The cross does not always remain the cross of shame. In the life of the Christ, the Holy One, the Son of God, it became glorified in having been overcome. Just so with us; each cross met, bravely borne, and overcome, becomes radiant with light and brings us into a more perfect understanding of the purpose of life and the glory that may be in the crown of life.

> There was a cross that fell on me with shadows
>   dark and long
> It crowded out my sun, my light, and blotted
>   out my song;
> But when I raised my eyes for help, I saw a
>   Radiant One,
> That stooped to lift my heavy cross—'Twas
>   Christ, the Blessed Son.[15]

Why Must I, as a Soul in a Material Plane, Bear a Cross?

This is a question that each of us individually should ask ourselves, and the manner in which we answer determines our spiritual status. It is the spiritual gauge of our development since the fall of man.

Whenever this question has been considered, many go away and walk no more in the way. "Will ye go also?"[16] Shall we not reply, "Lord, to whom shall we go? For Thou alone hast the words of eternal life." (See 262-35.) Shall we evade the cross that is ours to bear, especially at this time when mankind is entering the greatest test period in the history of the world? The words of the prophet seem to come ringing down the ages, "Who may abide the day

[14]Matt. 12:50   [15]P.E.   [16]P.R. See John 6:67

of His coming?"[17] Know we not that it is only those whose loins are girt about with truth? Who shall be able to abide to take this stand?

As individuals in the material plane, we must of necessity bear many things coincident with His earthly experience, and by recognizing our obligations as children of the living God, as He did, and learning from Him the lesson of meekness and lowliness of heart, we exemplify through service and sacrifice the life He lived.

Knowing that the purpose of life is to be one with the Father, we have to wait if we expect to see results in material manifestation. There is no surer way of realization than "to keep on keeping on"[18] in the way of the Christ. While our efforts may seem wrong in the eyes of everyone, there is a Power that takes hold in our extremities and adjusts every situation. As we trust that Power, our strength is renewed.

As we meet the crosses, endure the temptations, and overcome them, we become heirs and joint heirs with Him to the crown of glory. All who fulfill the purpose for which they are called bear their crosses not in sorrow, not in wailing, but in the joy of the Lord.

As a sign to us who have met our crosses and have overcome them, there comes that ability to meet other and greater crosses in the joy of the Lord, and to rejoice that we are counted worthy.

Let us enter into the service that may be our part as channels of blessings to others. In so doing we become conscious that our lives are spent in the way He would have us go, and that His presence abides with us. The door is open. Virtue and understanding find activity. Faith is renewed day by day, for we are more able to understand conditions that arise—whether from the mental, the material, or the spiritual. Access to the Father may be held as a cooperative force in whatever sphere of activity we may engage when in service to others.

It is not in times or seasons or in any place—but in every place, every day, and every hour that we may show forth His love to those we contact. By our lives others

[17]Mal. 3:2   [18]P.R. See also 364 series and 5749 series

may know that He walks with us and is our friend. Upon what is the glory of the crown conditioned? Faith-ful-ness.

Lesson XI

THE LORD THY GOD IS ONE

"For there is one God; and there is none other but He."
Mark 12:32

Affirmation

As my body, mind and soul are one, Thou, O Lord, in the manifestations in the earth, in power, in might, in glory, art one. May I see in that I do, day by day, more of that realization, and manifest the more.   *262-38*

XI

THE LORD THY GOD IS ONE

[Based on Edgar Cayce readings 262-38 through 262-42]

"Thou art One, the first of every number, and the
foundation of every structure.
Thou art One, and at the mystery of Thy Oneness the
wise of heart are struck dumb,
For they know not what it is.
Thou art One, and Thy Oneness can neither be
increased nor lessened;
It lacketh naught, nor doth aught remain over.
Thou art One, but not like a unit to be grasped or
counted,
For number and change cannot reach Thee.
Thou art not to be envisaged, nor to be figured thus and
thus . . ."   S.I.G.

Introduction

Unity is perhaps the most difficult truth that we have
to realize and manifest, although it is evinced all about
us. Through the mouth of His prophets, the Creator
repeatedly reminded His chosen ones, "Hear, O Israel,
the Lord our God is one Lord";[1] yet they, as other
nations, would wander away and seek other gods. In the
simplest and most comprehensible way, the Creator has
revealed to His creation His power, glory, and might.
"The word is very nigh unto thee, in thy mouth and in thy
heart, that thou mayest do it."[2] It is planted not only in
the heart, but "The heavens declare the glory of God; and
the firmament sheweth His handywork. Day unto day
uttereth speech, and night unto night sheweth knowl-

[1]Deut. 6:4   [2]Romans 10:8

edge. There is no speech nor language, where their voice is not heard."[3]

The Manifestations of God Are One

In the universe all manifestations are of God and are one with Him. In Him they live and move and have their being. This Supreme Intelligence that moves in the earth is manifested in the tiniest molecule as perfectly as in a great planet. How wonderful to realize that there is only one force, one power, one presence, and that is God, the Father. God is Spirit. "If I ascend up into heaven, Thou art there: if I make my bed in hell, behold, Thou art there. If I take the wings of the morning, and dwell in the uttermost parts of the sea; even there shall Thy hand lead me."[4]

As a pebble tossed into a lake sends out ripples that finally reach the farthest shore, just so do our acts, whether good or bad, affect others. As in our bodies, when a member is injured, the whole suffers, so do we as individuals influence the whole of society.

Our mental, physical, and spiritual bodies must be consecrated as channels for spiritual forces, if we would fully comprehend our duty to the whole and apply ourselves in working out the purposes of God. The Father has not willed that any should perish. All may come into the knowledge of their relationship to Him. When we realize this, obstacles become stepping-stones; our enemies (hindrances and weaknesses) become means through which we may mount to higher attainments.

Amid the turmoils of the present day, if we exercise patience, faith, the attributes of God, we have unparalleled opportunites to observe the Father working through His children. It is not necessary to have some great vision or experience, but just to be kind and to perform each task cheerfully. These are things of spirit and become proofs to us and the world that "My Father worketh hitherto, and I work."[5] The only thing that can separate us from this understanding is ourselves. We alone can open or shut the door.

We should never allow ourselves to feel separate and

[3]Psalm 19:1-3   [4]Psalm 139:8-10   [5]John 5:17

apart from God or our fellow man; for what affects our neighbor on the other side of the world affects us. The people of the earth are one great family. We should love without distinction, knowing that God is in all. By making ourselves perfect channels that His grace, mercy, peace, and love may flow through us, we come to realize more and more the Oneness of all creation. Let us keep the heart open that the voice of Him who has called may quicken every thought and act. His ways are not hidden nor far away, but are manifested to those who will hear and see the glory of the Oneness. Through the activity of the will is the method by which each of us should prepare himself as a channel for forces that may assist in gaining a greater concept of the Oneness of the Father in the material plane.

How We May Come into the Realization of the Oneness

We come into consciousness of the Oneness, not through any act of our own other than that we believe, trust, have faith, and come to realize that all material things are, in essence, spiritual. The Master said, "Ye are gods."[6] Does it not behoove us to take Him at His word and act the part? O, Thou who art God, present within each of us, forgive our unbelief! Let us pray for the greater realization of His presence. He is real, even as a brother at our side, and is faithful to keep His promises. As we are striving toward this realization, let us, moment by moment, be conscious that in every act, word, and deed His power is manifesting in and through us, and that there can be no separateness. We alone shut out the glories that may be our experiences in the realization of unity. Let us see to it that our lives, activities, thoughts, and meditations are more and more in accord with the will of the Father; for in so doing we become more Godlike and less selfish, and less of the carnal influences enter into our activities. We will then be in a position to teach others and will be on fire with the power that will manifest through us, and more and more at peace and in harmony with those experiences that are ours through

[6]John 10:34

our walks with Him in meditation and prayer.

How may we come into a realization of the Oneness? Take God at His word, "I am God, and beside me there is none other."[7] "Without me ye can do nothing."[8] Listen to the Voice and act upon it. Learn the lessons that nature teaches. Realize that the power within us is the God Force, the good force—although we, and we alone, through our wills may misuse it, causing it to become evil. If we will wait on the Lord, He will speak to us and will bring all things to our remembrance, even to the realization of our oneness with Him. Strive to see God in every one as well as in every thing. Meditate, pray, listen, and believe.

The At-Onement Through Jesus, the Christ

One of the basic and essential principles of Jesus' teachings is contained in the statement, "I and my Father are one."[9] It is to His life as an example and to His explanations of the Creative Force that we may turn with a feeling of complete faith for understanding. Jesus demonstrated in a very practical manner the Oneness of God as related to each individual soul. He showed us what could be attained by an individual who was willing to make his will one with that of the Father. He promised us that He would make intercession for us, opening a way for all who seek to be drawn to the Father.

In the simplicity of His life and teachings, Jesus brings to our understanding the fact that God is very near to us, that He is even within our own hearts. Much of the beauty and strength of His philosophy of life lies in the personal touch, in the direct connection which He establishes between man and his Creator.

Jesus' years of ministry were spent in practical demonstration of His consciousness of the Oneness of Creative Force. His words and acts were in compliance with the law which He understood so thoroughly. Whether it was on the open hillside before the masses, or in the seclusion of some quiet grove before a select few, He was ever explaining and demonstrating the truths which He knew

[7]P.R. See Isaiah 46:9   [8]John 15:5   [9]John 10:30

would make men truly free. He had walked the way and now chose to guide those who also sought a closer walk with the Creator.

Jesus learned obedience through suffering. He earned the right to be the Mediator for mankind; the right to guide those who seek in His name. If we will only follow the example He set, we will come into a realization of this truth, which He lived and taught, "The Lord our God is one Lord."[10]

As we strive to make ourselves in at-onement with Him, we must deny any other influence. He will bear us up and give us the help we need. There is power in His name. It is the symbol of attainment, understanding, and the realization of God's universal law (love). It is strength for those who are weary, peace to a troubled heart and mind. He is the Saviour to all who seek the at-onement.

Let us strive to realize more fully and show by our practical applications that we are workers together with God—that each of us, that each of God's creatures, is filling his niche in the great Oneness. From our point of view, it may be a very poor expression, but God sees deeper into each heart and knows all things.

The kind old lady who offers her simple herb to relieve the pain of the little child, and the skilled physician who is giving his best to mitigate the ills of mankind are as much in at-onement with Him as the saint who, with a touch of love, opens the eyes of the blind. Each is doing his part with the talent given into his keeping; each is working out his own development in his own way, which is the manifestation of His will.

The fullness of the realization of the Oneness of the Father was brought to His children when Jesus the Christ sent into the world the Holy Spirit. It is the Holy Spirit that brings to our remembrance all things.

Personal Experiences

"That the Father is One with His children has been demonstrated in my life many times, but ten years ago there was an incident that makes this truth stand out

[10]Deut. 6:4

more clearly to me than anything in my experience.

"My little boy was very sick. The physicians had done all in their power to help him, but their efforts appeared fruitless.

"We were living then near a church. My son, before his illness, played and talked, day after day, with the old sexton. They grew to be great friends, and the sexton loved him very dearly. He would often speak of how the child taught him lessons of forgiveness.

"One morning during the illness the sexton came to our home and asked to see the child. We led him to the room. He took off his working gloves and laid them aside, knelt by the bed and, with upturned face, began to talk with God. A new peace came into my heart. I knew that all was well. It took this saintly old man to teach me more perfectly than I had ever realized, that the Father works with those who will let Him, and can through them perform miracles."

A minister of state from a foreign country has all the rights of his country respected in the land to which he is an ambassador. He has the power to draw on his country for protection and in the name of his country demand it in his new home. Just so we are ambassadors in the earth, representatives of the King of kings, and while here we may claim all the power and protection of the kingdom from which we came, provided we are true representatives and are carrying out the mission for which we were sent.

The chief executive of a country can broadcast a message to his people. The message is for all, but only those who choose to tune in will hear it. Those who do not tune in are nonetheless a part of the whole, but their negligence indicates that they are unworthy of the interest that their chief has in them.

God has not changed. He seeks to awaken every human heart as of old. It is we who may close ourselves to the constant message of love ever in the Christ. Through prayer and meditation, we can attune ourselves to a clearer understanding and realization of His love and may receive the gift of the Spirit that would make us know, "I and my Father are one."[11]

God manifests in all He has created. Whether it be in the material plane—as demonstrated by radio; in the mental realm, as experienced through thought transference; or, in the spiritual awakening, as manifests in so-called religious experiences—all substance is one. Vibration may vary from the slow motion of matter to the invisible speed of thought. Only our points of perception and understanding change with our development. Let us realize that though we may be as one who has caught only the first glimpse of light as from the entrance of a dark cave, and who still stumbles blindly over dangerous rocks and beside deep pits, we are striving ever to reach the light of truth.

As we open our hearts to the unseen Forces that surround the throne of grace, mercy, and might, and throw about ourselves the protection found in the thought of the Christ, as we abide daily in the light of His teachings, so that every word, thought, and act are in harmony with the whole, we become more and more conscious of the Oneness. It is then we are privileged to hear His voice and know the comfort of His abiding presence.

Conclusion

Our God is a God of the physical, mental, and spiritual realms. Let us not lose sight of His activity in every plane and through every force. Our own desires and wills may sometimes blind us to the true requirements for adequate expression in any or all of these planes. We must constantly examine ourselves. In whatever plane of activity we may find ourselves, let us seek the most perfect expression of the God Force. Every atom of our physical bodies should vibrate in harmony. Our minds should be in constant touch with and filled with that which is stimulating and uplifting, guided and directed by a purpose to reach an ideal that is set in Him.

Let us not be discouraged; it is little by little, line upon line, that we grow in grace, in knowledge, and in the understanding of His ways. They are not hidden, nor far away, but are revealed to those who will hear and see the

[11]John 10:30

glory of the Oneness in the Father.

Let us examine ourselves to see how sincere is our desire to know that the Lord our God is One. Is it sufficient to be active rather than passive? If we would gain the concept, we must believe that He is, and that He rewards those who seek to do His will. He is life. We are to make our desires, our hearts, our minds, and our souls one with Him in bringing to the knowledge of all that the power of God, through the Christ, is able to cause us to know that "there is one God; and there is none other but He: and to love Him with all the heart, and with all the understanding, and with all the soul, and with all the strength, and to love his neighbor as himself, is more than all whole burnt offerings and sacrifices."[12]

> As my body, mind and soul are one, Thou, O Lord, in the manifestations in the earth, in power, in might, in glory, art one. May I see in that I do, day by day, more of that realization, and manifest the more.   *262-38*

[12]Mark 12:32-33

Lesson XII

LOVE

"And now abideth faith, hope, love, these three; but the greatest of these is love."   1 Corinthians 13:13 [RV]

Affirmation

Our Father, through the love that Thou has
manifested in the world through Thy Son, the Christ,
make us more aware of "God is love."   *262-43*

XII

LOVE

[Based on Edgar Cayce readings 262-43 through 262-48]

Introduction

Love is God. The whole law is fulfilled in these three words. Mankind is urged to observe and to cultivate this attribute, for it is through love that physical life is perfected and the continuity of life realized. Life is Creative Force in action and is the expression of love.

Love, divine love, is universal. It is found in the smile of a babe, which indeed is love undefiled, in the beauty of a song, and in a soul raised in praise to the Giver of Light. There is love manifested in the performance of duty when there is no thought of personal gain, in speaking encouraging words to those seeking an understanding, and in the activities of those doing their best with the talents entrusted to them. Love may be found in a contented heart that is willing to wait until the time is fulfilled when the ideal may be realized. Love that passes understanding is found in His Consciousness.

Love Manifested

It is the privilege of every soul to find joy in communing with God in nature; for each creation is a complete unit of expression of the Creative Power.

Christ perfectly manifested the love of the Maker. His life and teachings are the inspiration for the regeneration of all mankind. As sons of God we can manifest God's love if we allow Him to have His way in our lives.

Joy comes through service even in toil and pain. Pure, undefiled love is so powerful that men may lay down their lives for others. Self is forgotten.

> Then, come ye, my children! Harken unto that which thou hast attained in thine self, that ye may put on the whole armor and be fruitful in the love of Him [who] calls that *everyone* should hear, should know, should understand, that God is in His heavens and that His love endureth even to those who harden their hearts— and wills that no one should perish; rather that in the love as may be manifested in the daily walks, the daily activities of every soul, each may show through that manifested the love which impels the giving of everything within self as a manifestation of He, the Master, having spoken with thee!   262-44

The Power of Love

Love is the force that uplifts and inspires mankind. Children starve without it. Men and women wither and decay when it is lacking. It costs nothing, yet its value cannot be measured by material standards. It can lift a wretched human being from the miry clay of despair and set his feet upon the solid rock of respectability and service.

Love is that inexplicable force which brought Jesus to earth so that through Him the way back to the Father might be made plain to the children of men. It caused the Father to give His Son that whosoever believes might have eternal life. Love is that dynamic force which brings into manifestation all things. It is the healing force, the cleansing force, and the force that blesses all things we touch. With our hearts filled with love we will see only goodness and purity in everybody and in everything. In the beginning love looked upon the earth and saw that it was good and blessed it.

As love is God, it is, therefore, our abundant supply. Do we lack? Do we love? Do we allow conditions to keep us from the realization of the presence of God? If so, how can we expect the flow of abundance, when we are keeping the channel blocked by our thoughts and attitudes? We are standing in the way of our own success.

When conditions arise which seem hard to endure, if we would realize that we are workers together with God and that each condition is perhaps some problem in our lives that must be met and overcome, we might stop and count our blessings instead of counting our hardships. Only with our hearts filled with love—love for conditions, love for people, love for God—can we fuly realize this. Life is growth. We never can grow in knowledge and understanding and really be channels of blessings until we have endured and conquered in ourselves just the things that we would help others to overcome. Love allows no place for hate and recognizes no evil, but sees all things working together for good. The power of love is unlimited. We alone may set the metes and bounds. We may use it constructively or selfishly. We may uplift our fellow man or crush ideals, instigate revolts, and wreck civilization. It all depends upon whether we are in love with ourselves or are willing to lay down our lives for others.

The Test of Love

"Love suffereth long, and is kind ... beareth all things, believeth all things, hopeth all things, endureth all things."[1] Can we truthfully say, "I am persuaded, that neither death, nor life, nor angels, nor principalities, nor powers, nor things present, nor things to come, nor height, nor depth, nor any other creature, shall be able to separate us from the love of God, which is in Christ Jesus our Lord?"[2] The Master said, "This is my commandment, that ye love one another, as I have loved you."[3] Greater love hath no man than this, that a man lay down his life for his friends."[4] "Love your enemies ... that ye may be the children of your Father which is in heaven: for He maketh his sun to rise on the evil and on the good, and sendeth rain on the just and on the unjust."[5] He that does not love his worst enemy has not even begun to develop. The Father's love is the golden thread, that is woven throughout the Scriptures, which enlarges and spreads until the whole law is fulfilled in "God so loved the world, that he gave his only begotten Son, that whosoever believeth in him should not perish, but have everlasting

[1] I Cor. 13:4, 7 [RV] [2] Romans 8:38-39 [3] P.R. See John 13:34
[4] John 15:13 [5] Matt. 5:44, 45

life."[6] To fulfill the law of love is more than simply to love those who love us, for by so doing we have not reached the faintest conception of divine love.

Love is giving out the best that is within us. Then, where slights, slurs, or even suspicions have been allowed to affect us, love cannot mean all that it should in our experience. The Master asks of us that we love Him, that we keep His commandments that He may abide with us, even as He abides with the Father. All of us believe, all know, and all understand that those things that hinder are caused by selfishness. This prevents even the dawn of the concept of what love should mean to us. Few of us have found the love that makes us free indeed, that keeps us from making unkind remarks, and prevents us from being disappointed in things, in people, and in conditions. How much are we willing to bear, to do, and to suffer that others may become aware of the love of the Father?

Love Is Giving

The law of love does not do away with other laws, but makes the law of recompense, the law of faith, the law of earth forces of effect—not defective but effective. Love is that attribute of the soul that enables us to give, asking nothing in return. Christ exemplified this in His life, in His death, and in His parting promise after His resurrection, "Lo, I am with you alway, even to the end of the age."[7] If mankind could get the vision of what it means to love as He loves, what peace would come on earth!

Do we want the best for another before our own wants and desires are satisfied? Can we see some good in all whom we meet? This is the Christ way of showing love. Where we are weak, He is ready to sympathize, comfort, and supply strength. In His name there is power. If we call on His name, if we abide in His teachings, we will radiate such a glow of righteousness (right thinking and acting) that those who sit in darkness will see great light.

Let us take hold on things of the spirit, for they alone are eternal. "The children of Light are called even now into service that His day may be hastened, lest many

[6]John 3:16   [7]P.R. See Matt. 28:20

faint."[8] Do we not remember our years and years of service for our families and for our friends, in which every act was so prompted by love that there was never a thought of being weary? When our best years have been spent for them and we are no longer needed or seemingly appreciated, does sadness fill our hearts? Let us not forget that such service is never lost, for with love it has been woven into the souls of those for whom we worked. It will shine forth again and again in the lives of many yet unborn. Love never dies; it is eternal.

Divine Love Passes Understanding

Undoubtedly, the reason that mankind does not totally accept the way back to the Father, made perfect through the Christ, is that so great a love as the Father showed forth for His children passes understanding. God, the Father, the First Cause, in the manifestations of Self brought the world, as we observe it about us, into being through love. He gave to man, His creation, the ability to become one with Him. This way was shown through the Christ, the Mediator with the Father. Hence we realize that God so loved the world that He gave His only begotten Son, that we through Him might have life—God more abundant.

> ..."Ye that have known me knoweth my Father also, for I am in Him, and ye in me"—may know that love that maketh the life burn as an ember in a darkened and unregenerated world. "For unto me must come all that would find the way. I *am* the Way. Ye are my brethren. Ye have been begotten in the flesh through the love made manifest in the earth." Then, in the spirit and in the mind that hast brought thee to that understanding and consciousness of His love made manifest, abide ye day by day.   262-44

Personal Experiences

"I was seeking to know and experience that love that passes understanding. I soon found that if I would love I must know Him who is the Author of Love. The way was pointed out to me: Commune the more often in the inner shrine, in the Holy of Holies. Meet the presence of the

[8]P.R.

Father there; know the love of the Christ in action; experience and see the power of the Holy Spirit."

"In meditation I found the peace that I had been seeking for months. It was not far away, but very near, even within my heart. I came to know that my Redeemer lives, that His presence may be experienced, and that my body, mind, and soul may be one with Him."

"In a trying experience I sought divine love. I realized more and more the consciousness of the presence of the Father and the consolation that I was being watched over by guardian angels. Peace filled my soul. 'Herein is love, not that we loved God, but that He loved us, and sent His Son to be the propitiation for our sins.' "[9]

"I have found that in sending out thoughts of love to any person or thing the whole environment may be changed. My child was very cross one night. She did not want to study or obey any of my requests. I began to look at her and send her thoughts of love. She seemed to get them very quickly, for in a short while her face was wreathed in smiles, and without further trouble she came to the table and began to study. Instantly, her whole attitude changed to one of obedience. Not a word was said; love alone conquered."

"The law that brought worlds into existence is the same law that makes us friends with all of God's creatures. My children were great lovers of pets and were ready to adopt any they found homeless or friendless. My experience deals with a homeless cat which made frequent visits to our back yard. She was so wild that she would run if she saw or heard anyone approach. We would leave food for her, but she was so filled with fear that she did not dare let us see her eat it.

"By our constant kindness in caring for her and showing our love, for we had come to love and pity her, she finally dropped her fear and would let us pet her, and if permitted would even come into the house. It took two years to accomplish this, but we succeeded. Truly, 'Love casteth out fear.' "[10]

The power of love may work in the lives of individuals in material ways as well as spiritual, as indicated in the

[9]I John 4:10   [10]See I John 4:18

following experience.

"Someone that I dearly loved was in need of financial help. One morning when it seemed I had on me all I could bear, from a material standpoint, he came to me and asked for a loan of a hundred dollars. I felt that he was asking for my all, as I had only a little more in the bank from which I could draw and did not know when I would be able to get more. It seemed as if I were a child and someone had asked for my last penny, which I wanted very much.

"In my dilemma, the thought came to me that I could not reject my friend, but should go to the bank and let him have it, for his mental distress outweighed my desire for self-preservation. There followed many constructive as well as conflicting thoughts. Should I take almost all I had and give to another? Was I called on to make such a sacrifice? Finally, there came to me a realization of the great sacrifice made for me, and the love of the Heavenly Father for His children. My conflicting thoughts vanished and I had peace. For had He not promised, 'I will never leave thee, nor forsake thee'?[11]

"The power of love is slowly molding the lives of us all. I know this because of its influence in helping me day by day to show forth His love and to live in the way that He may be glorified through my service to others."

Conclusion

Come ye, my children, in that ye have all been called unto that way which would show forth to thy neighbor, thy brethren, that the Father loved His children. Who *are* His children? They that keep His commandments day by day. For unto him that is faithful and true is given the crown of life. The harvest is ripe, the laborers are few. Be not weary because there has been that which has *seemed* to trouble thee, for the ways are being opened to those that show themselves faithful and true. Faint not, for the day of the Lord is near at hand.   *262-47*

Our Father, through the love that Thou hast manifested in the world through Thy Son, the Christ, make us more aware of "God is love."   *262-43*

[11]Hebrews 13:5

GOD IS LOVE

"If I speak with the tongues of men and of angels, but have not love, I am become sounding brass, or a clanging cymbal. And if I have the gift of prophecy, and know all mysteries and all knowledge; and if I have all faith, so as to remove mountains, but have not love, I am nothing. And if I bestow all my goods to feed the poor, and if I give my body to be burned, but have not love, it profiteth me nothing. Love suffereth long, and is kind; love envieth not; love vaunteth not itself, is not puffed up, doth not behave itself unseemly, seeketh not its own, is not provoked, taketh not account of evil; rejoiceth not in unrighteousness, but rejoiceth with the truth; beareth all things, believeth all things, hopeth all things, endureth all things. Love never faileth: but whether there be prophecies, they shall be done away, whether there be tongues, they shall cease; whether there be knowledge, it shall be done away. For we know in part, and we prophesy in part: but when that which is perfect is come, that which is in part shall be done away. When I was a child, I spake as a child, I felt as a child, I thought as a child: now that I am become a man, I have put away childish things. For now we see in a mirror, darkly; but then face to face: now I know in part; but then shall I know even as also I have been known. But now abideth faith, hope, love, these three; and the greatest of these is love."   *I Corinthians 13 [RV]*

A.R.E.® STUDY GROUP PROGRAM

The *A Search for God* books were written by the original members of the first study group. While individuals who are not in an A.R.E. study group will find this book valuable to their personal growth in consciousness, the information contained in the two slim volumes of *A Search for God* provides a unique, step-by-step growth sequence of lessons, and the books are best utilized in a group climate.

The four basic tools in A.R.E. group work are:

1. Study of *A Search for God* material edited by the Cayce source
2. Group meditation (and individual meditation each day at the same time)
3. Daily prayer for each member of the group
4. Group applications of "disciplines"—weekly projects to apply the studied material.

There are 1,500 such group meetings in every state, many Canadian provinces, and foreign countries around the world. If you would like to know more about the exciting group process that can change your life, write to:

A.R.E. Study Group Department
215 67th Street
Virginia Beach, VA 23451-2061

and we will be happy to send you the names of an A.R.E. *Search for God*® Group in your area.

BIBLIOGRAPHY OF RECOMMENDED PARALLEL MATERIAL

(Available directly from A.R.E. Press, 215 67th Street, Virginia Beach, VA 23451-2061; write for catalog.)

A Search for God, Book I
A Search for God, Book II
The Handbook for A.R.E. Study Groups
Edgar Cayce and Group Dynamics
Experiments in a Search for God: The Edgar Cayce Path of Application
Experiments in Practical Spirituality
There Is a River (biography of Edgar Cayce)

The transcriptions of the original readings (from which the *A Search for God* books were distilled) given to the first study group and prayer group are also available as companion texts:

Library Series, Volume 2, *Meditation, Part I* (Prayer Group Readings)
Library Series, Volume 7, *Study Group Readings* (from which *A Search for God* text was compiled)

Index and Glossary of Terms

Abraham: One who is called Lord thy God is One Lord"

Akashic Records: A vibratory record of all thought and action

At-Onement: Perfect attunement with the Father; 128

Attributes of God: Love, mercy, virtue, etc.; 13-49, 65-135

Awakening: Spiritual awareness; 26-45

Body: Physical, mental, spiritual; 7-33

Breathing: Meditation; 17

Center, Vibratory: Meditation; 9

Christ Consciousness: The Holy Spirit; 45

Christ, Mind of: Service; 26

Confidence: 49-50

Cooperation: 25-30

Creative Energy: God; Meditation; 25-59

Cross and Crown: 111

Entity: 33

Evil: 142

Faith: 49-55

Fellowship: 69-78

Force: All force is one; "The

Force, Evil: Good misused

Fourth Dimension: A state of consciousness in which the limitations of time and space are removed; 36

God: Creative Energy; Universal Mind; Universal Force; Father; Lord; Jehovah; Allah; Yah; etc.; 69

Glands: Meditation; 9

Glory: The privilege to serve

Grace: God's free love

Group Purpose: To serve

Healing: Meditation

Holy Spirit: God in action

Idea: A result of mental activity in the physical plane (not to be confused with *ideal* in studying the lessons); 43

Ideal: A perfect spiritual goal outside of self to which one would attain; 43

Immortality: Generally applied to the existence of the soul after death; more accurately this might be applied to the "eternal existence of the soul"

Israel: Those who seek

Judgment: Reaction to compliance with or breaking of spiritual, mental, or physical laws

Judgment Day: A checking up on the progress of the spiritual development of a soul-entity

Love: "God is Love"; 135-142

Lamb of God: The Christ

Leydig, Cells of: Meditation; 9

Light: Awareness of the spiritual purpose of the universe

Meditation: 5-21

Michael: An archangel; Lord of the Way; 107

Mind: An attribute of God; a power given to men; 5

Oneness: The Lord thy God is One; 125-132

Open Door: 91-98

Patience: 81-87

Pituitary Gland: 9

P.E.: Personal experience of a member of the study group

P.R.: Psychic reading (when possible, the individual case number of the specific Edgar Cayce reading is noted)

Presence, In His: 101-108

Readings: Recorded oral discourses given by Edgar Cayce while in superconscious state

Self: Know Thyself; 33-40

Senses: The five physical senses

Soul: That part of us that is made in the image of God

Truth, Spirit of: 36

Virtue and Understanding: 59-65

Will: The power of choice given us by God; freedom of the will is one of the basic principles explained in the lessons and readings; 24

Word (made flesh): Christ; 117